Pascal Bruno
by Alexandre Dumas

PASCAL BRUNO.

A SICILIAN STORY.

Dumas, Alexandre (Davy)

EDITED BY

THEODORE HOOK, ESQ.

"Disguised—discovered—conquering—ta'en—condemned."
BYRON.

LONDON:

HENRY COLBURN, PUBLISHER,

13, GREAT MARLBOROUGH STREET.

1837.

WHITING, BEAUFORT HOUSE, STRAND.

INTRODUCTION.

My attention was drawn to the following story by a kind and highly-valued friend (to whom *par parenthese* I beg to dedicate this version of it), who was much struck by the wildness and originality of its construction. It is from the pen of M. Alexander Dumas, and has appeared periodically in one of the French journals.

M. Dumas prefaces it in the original, by informing his reader, that there are four ways of getting to Sicily from Naples.

The first mode of proceeding is by se-
curing a place in the steam-packet, which,
however, has no fixed day for sailing, but
is delayed until a sufficient number of
passengers are collected, to make it worth
the owner's while to undertake the voyage.

The second course to be adopted, is
to go in the *Malle Poste* through Calabria
to Reggio, whence there are passage-boats
crossing to Messina every hour. If this
is not agreeable, you have only to make
a bargain with some coach-master, who
will carry you by the same route, stopping
to sleep every night. The fourth method
is to hire a small sailing-boat to take you
to Palermo, for which you pay six ducats
per diem; in consideration of which, you
have the vessel entirely to yourself, and
with the crew, captain, and all, completely
under your own command.

In the steam-packet, you make the trip in four-and-twenty hours; in the *Malle Poste*, it occupies a week. In your hired carriage you arrive in about a fortnight; and in the sailing-boat, when God pleases. " Notwithstanding its uncertainty," says M. Dumas, "we preferred the latter, especially as we were tempted by a fair and fresh breeze. Providence, however, upon this special occasion, was bounteous overmuch. The breeze increased to a gale, and we were at anchor in the port of Messina on the evening of the third day."

" So perfectly satisfied were we with our voyage and our vessel, which behaved admirably as a sea-boat, and so very much pleased with the skill and coolness of her captain, and the activity and willingness of his crew, whenever their courage or services were required, that instead of discharging her we made a fresh bargain, and instead of traversing the island on shore, resolved on making a coasting voyage round it in our favourite spero-nare." .

It was during this voyage, which lasted upwards of six weeks, that the author and his friend heard the captain and some of the crew frequently speaking of wild and startling events, connected with the village of Bauso and one Pascal Bruno, of whom they told strange stories, and to whom, as it appeared, they attributed some superhuman power. These fragments of his history awakened the curiosity and excited the interest of the voyagers so much, that they took the first opportunity of landing, in order to visit the scene of his exploits, and accordingly hired a little carriage at Messina for three ducats for the day, started at nine o'clock the following morning and reached Bauso by noon.

When they arrived there, Pietro, one of the crew of the speronare, a native of Bauso, who accompanied them, proceeded to the house of a notary, whom he knew to be in possession of all the authenticated documents respecting Pascal Bruno, and mentioning the anxiety of the travellers to be made acquainted with them, the worthy old gentleman paid them a visit after breakfast, and kindly placed at the author's disposal a mass of papers from the contents of which the following history was collated.

M. Dumas has given some beautiful descriptions of Sicily—a lengthened narrative of the voyage, and one or two interesting stories collected during its continuance. Pascal Bruno has, however, absorbed my attention and I pass over all the rest. Amongst other motives which have led me to publish it, is a hope that some of the scenes and situations described in its pages, may be thought worthy of illustration by the inimitable Cattermole, a circumstance which would ensure new gratification to the British public, and a new triumph to British art.

T. E. H.

LONDON,
Oct. 1, 1837.

PASCAL BRUNO.

CHAPTER I.

IF ever city on the face of the earth were predestined to be blest, that city is Palermo — founded upon a fruitful soil, beneath a cloudless sky, and washed by an azure sea. The hill of St. Rosalia shelters it from the north wind, while Cape Naferino shields it from the malign influence of the eastern blast. The vast plain on which it stands is protected by a chain of mountains, which forms its belt.

B

The changes of government which Palermo has experienced have wrought no change in *her*——she still remains in all her native purity and brightness——her various masters have been tempted by her charms, but she continues unaltered, and appears even to have gained new beauties from their chains, which, however well they may record their conquests, seem only to add additional ornaments to their lovely slave.

Thus it is that art and nature, time and circumstances, events and men, have conspired to embellish and decorate her. From the Greeks she derives her temples, from the Romans her aqueducts. The Saracens have bequeathed her their castles; the Normans their cathedrals; while to the Spaniards she is indebted for her churches. Adorned with

these beautiful relics, of every age, and
of every nation, Palermo (thanks to her
delightful climate) blossoms and blooms
in all the fragrance and gaiety of nature.
There the palm of Egypt bends to the
gentle breeze, beside its sturdy neigh-
bour, the gnarled oak of England, and
the Indian fig offers its melting tribute,
intertwined with the fir of Scotland.

Those who, for the first time, have
revelled in the sparkling clearness of a
Sicilian day little anticipate the transport
to be obtained over their senses and
feelings of a Sicilian night. The nights
at Palermo baffle description ; the pure,
balmy, and almost brilliant atmosphere,
the breath of zephyrs, and the gentle
murmur of the restless wave, that breaks
upon the shore, mingled with the not
" busy hum of men" within the city,

blend, as it were, in one sweet har-
mony of universal love.

But, is this picture always bright—are
these allurements constantly without alloy
—is this most lovely of cities free from
evil ? Alas, no ! Nature in this favoured
land will have her way. On a sudden
the bright scene is changed ; the sea
assumes a livid hue—the gay town is
mute. A drift of clouds to the north-
ward announces the approach of the
Sirocco, the Khamsin of Arabia ; a
burning mist, rising from the Libyan
sands, and wafted to Europe upon the
south-eastern wind. Its effect is pesti-
lential; the young, the aged, the rich,
the poor, the healthful, and the sick,
bend before its dreadful influence. The
calamity is universal, the brute beasts
feel its awful power equally with their

lords and masters, and all sink into a state of weakness, lassitude, and wretchedness; and this continues until a purer air, wafted from Calabria, resuscitates the languishing inhabitants, who recover from the baleful effects of the blast as those who have swooned, awake to luxury and pleasure.

One of these siroccoes had lasted throughout one day in September, 1803, and all its concomitant miseries had been endured in Palermo, but at sunset the sky cleared, the sea resumed its wonted clearness, and fresh breezes blew from the Lipari Islands. As usual, the influence of the blessed change was felt by all existing beings, and, as if newly created in that Eden of the world, the inhabitants roused themselves from their torpor.

At this moment, reader, start with me from Palermo, by St. George's Gate, leaving the castle of San Marco to the right, go direct to the Mole; then along by the track till you come to a villa situated on the edge of the sea, but whose beautiful gardens reach to the foot of Mount Pelegrino; that villa belongs to the Prince de Carini, the Viceroy of Ferdinand the Fourth of Sicily.

In that villa reposed, on a sofa, her head thrown back, and her hair dishevelled, a woman, beautiful beyond expression; so beautiful that, as she lay, pale and almost inanimate, she might have been mistaken for a lovely statue. A slight shuddering agitates her frame, the life-blood mounts to her cheek, her eyes open languidly, and a sweet sigh parts her rosy lips; she stretches out her fair hand to reach a little silver bell, placed on a table near her, rings it, and, as if fatigued by the exertion, sinks again upon her couch.

The watchful waiting-maid, young and pretty, hears the summons, a door of the apartment opens, and the disordered state of the gentle Teresa's dress proclaims that she, like her lady, had sunk beneath the oppressive influence of the Sirocco.

"Is that Teresa?" asked the lady, turning her head towards her. "Will the Sirocco last for ever?"

"Pardon, my lady," said Teresa, " it *has* subsided. People begin to breathe again."

" Bring me some fruit," said the lady, "some ice, and above all, give me some air."

Teresa obeyed, as speedily as her yet unconquered lassitude permitted; and placing the refreshments on the table, opened a window which commanded a view of the sea.

"Look countess," said Teresa, "we shall have fine weather to-morrow—the air is so clear, that although it is near sunset one can see the island of Alicari quite plainly."

"Ah!" said the countess, "the breeze indeed refreshes me; give me your arm, Teresa, I will endeavour to reach the window."

The countess merely tasted the sherbet, and leaning on the shoulder of her pretty attendant, feebly tottered to the balcony.

"Ah!" sighed she, inhaling the evening gale, "how much restored I feel already by this delightful breeze! Bring

me the cushion, and open the window
that faces the garden. Is the prince
returned from Montreal?"

" Not yet, madam," said the faithful
attendant.

" I do not regret his absence," said the
countess, " I would rather he should not
find me looking so wretchedly pale and
ill, as I am sure I do."

" I never," said Teresa, " saw your
ladyship look more beautiful. Well
may all the ladies of Palermo be jealous
of you."

" Come, Teresa," said the countess,
" this is absurd. What do you think of
the Marchesa Rudini or the Princess
Butera."

" I except no one," said the waiting-
maid.

" I really begin to suspect," said the

countess, "that the prince bribes you to praise me."

"And I assure *you*, madam," said Teresa, "that I only express my own sincere opinion in what I say."

"Well," said the countess, "it is certainly very delightful to live in Palermo."

"Particularly," said Teresa, "if one happens to be about two-and-twenty years old, and rich and beautiful."

"You merely anticipated the conclusion of my sentence," said the countess, "yet still I cannot be happy unless I am able to impart happiness to those around me. When are you to be married, Teresa?"

Teresa cast her eyes upon the floor and said nothing.

"Is not Sunday the day fixed?" asked the countess.

" It is, madam," replied the maid with a deep sigh.

" What then," said the countess, " have you not *quite* made up your mind, Teresa?"

' Yes, madam," said Teresa, " all is settled."

" You speak, Teresa," said the countess, " as if your heart and your hand were not to go together. Do you not love Gaetano?"

" I believe," said Teresa, her eyes still cast down, " that Gaetano is a well-disposed young man, and that he will do all in his power to make me happy; besides I am sure I shall be happy, because, by marrying him, I ensure to myself the happiness of remaining in your service."

" But why then do you sigh, Teresa?" asked the countess.

"Thoughts of home, madam," said Teresa, "and the recollections of *our* country will steal into the mind."

"*Our* country?" said the countess.

"Yes," replied the maid, "I may venture to say *our* country; since your ladyship sent for me from the village of which your noble father had been lord."

"Indeed you may," said the countess, "being my foster-sister."

"At the time I got your ladyship's kind summons," said Teresa, with some emotion, "I was on the eve of marriage to a young man of Bauso."

"Why did you not tell me this before, Teresa?" said her mistress. "If I had known it, I am sure the Prince would have taken him into his household, and then you could have remained with me as you will now do."

"Ah!" sighed Teresa, "he is too proud to be a servant."

"Indeed!" said the countess.

"Yes, my lady," said Teresa, "he had before I left Bauso, refused a situation in the household of the Prince de Goto."

"What," said the countess, smiling, "is he some nobleman in disguise?"

"No," replied Teresa, "he is a simple mountaineer."

"And pray, Teresa, what may be his name?" asked the countess.

"Oh," replied Teresa, hastily, "you would not know him if I told your ladyship; and, besides, I do not wish it to be mentioned."

"And you lament his loss?" asked the countess.

"Yes I do," sighed Teresa. "Although if I had married *him*, instead of marrying

Gaetano, I must have worked hard for my living, which perhaps I am not quite strong enough to do, and above all I must have left your ladyship; and then, even if I had got another place, I could never have found a lady so kind and so good-natured as you have been."

"And yet," said the countess, sadly, "I am accused of pride and arrogance— is that true, Teresa ?"

"I can bear testimony to your lady-ship's goodness to me," replied Teresa.

"The nobility of Palermo," said the countess, "call me presuming, because the family of Castel-Nuovo, was enno-bled by Charles the Fifth, while the Ventimilles and Partannas, date back to Tancred and Ruggiero; but the adventitious difference of birth, is not the real cause of their jealousy. They who affect to despise, envy me the affections of the Viceroy; yet all their efforts to alienate the love of Rodolfo are vain. Carini praises my superior beauty—and so do you, hypocrite."

"There is a still greater flatterer," said Teresa, "than either his Excellency or me."

"Indeed, Teresa!" said the countess, "and who may that be?"

"Your looking-glass, madam," said the fair waiting-maid.

"Silly child!" replied the lady—a smile of gratified vanity playing over her beautiful countenance. "Light the tapers of my *Psyche* — and shut this window—there is air enough from the other—and then, leave me."

Teresa obeyed — she had scarcely quitted the room, when the countess threw herself upon a chair before the mirror, and gazed with pleasure and

self-satisfaction on the beautiful form
she saw reflected thence.

This Emma, or Gemma, as she had
been from childhood called by her
family, by virtue of which addition
she sometimes called herself Diamante,
was in truth a lovely creature. Her
beauty was of a style and character
which are to be found nowhere except in Sicily, where a bright variety of
charms unite in one person. She might
have claimed to be descended from an
Athenian orator, a Saracenic emir, or a
Norman chief; for while her symme-
trical figure possessed an Ionian grace
and flexibility, her full orbed eyes
beamedwith Arabian brightness, and on
her fair and fervid cheek, glowed all
the health and gracefulness of France.

Pleased beyond her hopes with the
radiancy of her charms, she sought no

aid of art to heighten their attractions, but sank Narcissus-like into an abstracted admiration of herself, full rather of gratitude to Heaven for having made her so beautiful, than of vanity that she was so.

Gemma judged rightly ; what artificial accessory, could have given increased effect to the long raven-like ringlets, which fell loosely over her shoulders? what pencil could have improved the arch of her dark brow? what tint could have freshened the coral of her lips? None. And thus she sat musing, lost in a world of thoughts, sealed to all other minds and hearts but hers. The glass placed near the open window, reflected the bright firmament of Heaven, and Gemma amused herself by counting in her faithful mirror, the stars as they gradually appeared in the clear and cloudless sky.

c

All on a sudden the light was obscured—a dark shadow flitted before her — Gemma turned quickly round, and beheld a man standing in the balcony—Gemma sprang from her chair, and would have screamed for help, but the stranger leaped into the room, and clasping his hands, exclaimed,

"For mercy's sake, spare me!—fear nothing—I come not here to harm you."

Gemma overpowered by the surprise, as well as by the tone and manner of this appeal, sank back upon her chair, and cast a hurried but searching glance at the unexpected and unknown intruder.

He appeared to be about five or six and twenty years of age, and of the lower order. He wore a Calabrian hat, with a velvet band which fell over his shoulder; his dress was also of velvet, ornamented with silver buttons. His waist was encircled by one of those imitations of the fringed and embroidered Turkish belts, which are made at Messina. Gaiters and shoes completed his mountain costume, which was by no means inelegant, and seemed to have been adopted by the wearer on the present occasion, as peculiarly becoming. There was a savage beauty in the expression of his countenance; his features were strongly marked, and in his eyes, there was a haughty fierceness. His hair and beard were black.

It must be confessed, that Gemma gained no encrease of confidence by her rapid examination of her visiter's appearance, and she stretched forth her hand towards the silver bell that rested on her table.

"Did you not understand me, madam?" asked the stranger, in a tone of softness, which the voice of a Sicilian can so readily assume. "Assure yourself of perfect safety — I have come hither to make a request—grant me *that*, and I will worship you for your goodness."

"What is the nature of your request?" said Gemma, in a trembling accent. "Why have you broken in upon me at such a time as this?"

"Forgive me, lady," said the stranger, "had I presumed to ask an interview, you probably would not have condescended to accede to such a petition, coming from a poor and unknown person. Besides, even had you admitted me to your presence, you might have hesitated to answer my question, and I have no time to lose."

"Tell me then, at once," said Gemma,

somewhat assured by the manner of her visiter. "What is it you require of me?"

"In *your* keeping, madam," said the stranger, "are my hopes, my fears, my happiness, my misery, my life, my death."

"Explain," said Gemma, again startled by the earnestness of his manner.

"You have," said the stranger, "in your service a young woman from Bauso."

"Teresa?" said the countess.

"Yes, Teresa," replied the stranger, in a tremulous voice; "she is on the eve of marriage with one of Prince Carini's valets. She is my affianced wife."

"What!" exclaimed the countess, "are you"——

"Yes," interrupted the stranger, somewhat hastily, "I am the man. I, who was on the point of marrying her when she received your letter summoning her hither. She obeyed your command, and left me; but she vowed to remain true and constant, and to mention me to you favourably, and if she failed in her intercession, she promised to return. I believed her. I expected her; day by day I waited for her; night by night I watched; I wandered east and west, and south and north, and again returned to Bauso in quest of her; but she came not back. Three years had passed, when I resolved to seek her, and here I am. I have learned the whole truth since my arrival in Palermo. It was then, I resolved to throw myself at your feet and implore you to give me back the loved one of my heart."

" Of Teresa," said the countess, " I am extremely fond; she is indispensable to my comfort. I cannot part from her; and by marrying Gaetano, who is a favourite with the Prince, she will remain with me here."

" If entering the service of the Prince," said the stranger, " be the required condition of my happiness—I—*I* am ready to become his servant."

" Teresa told me," said the countess, " that you would never accept such a situation."

" Teresa is right," replied the stranger, " she knows my feelings, but she does not even yet appreciate my love : for *her* I *will* make the sacrifice."

" I will mention you to the Prince," said the countess. " If he consent"——

" If !" exclaimed the stranger ;" the world knows that with *him*, your wishes are commands."

" But," said the countess, " what security have I for your character."

" My eternal gratitude," replied the stranger."

" Still," said the fair Gemma, " it is necessary that I should know who you are."

" Suffice it," said the stranger, " that I am one whose destinies are at your disposal."

" Yet," said the countess, "the Prince will naturally ask your name."

" Why should he ?" said the stranger, " the name of an humble peasant from Bauso cannot be of much importance to his Excellency.

" But," said the countess, smiling graciously, " I am a countrywoman of yours. My father was the Count de Castel-Nuovo, possessed of the castle which stands not more than a quarter of a league from your birth-place."

"Yes," said the stranger, gloomily, his eyes resting sullenly on the fair form of the countess, "I know *that*."

"Well, then," said the countess, "I most probably have heard of your name; if I am to be a pleader in your cause, why not tell me?"

"Better you should never know it, madam," said the stranger. "What matters my name? I am an honest man, ready to make my Teresa happy; give her to me, and henceforward you and the Prince may command my life."

"Your silence is strange," said the countess, "and rendered more curious by the fact, that Teresa herself has positively refused to tell me who you are. Now, without knowing that, I repeat, it will be impossible for me to do you the least service."

"For the last time," said the stranger,

" I entreat—I warn you not to press me upon this point."

" In spite of which," said the countess, I must insist upon my condition ; tell me your name, or go."

The stranger's blanched cheek and heaving chest alone gave evidence of the emotion under which he laboured. He replied calmly.

" PASCAL BRUNO."

" Pascal Bruno !" almost shrieked the countess, as she recoiled from him, "Pascal Bruno, the son of the culprit Antonio Bruno, whose head is still exposed in an iron cage at the castle of Bauso ?"

" I am *his* son," said Pascal, without moving a muscle.

" Are you aware," said Gemma, " why his head is so exposed ?"

Pascal remained silent.

" Then I must tell you," said Gemma, " it is because *your* father attempted to murder *mine*?"

" I know *that*," said Pascal, " and I know that, when you were a child, your nurses showed you the head, and told *you* that, which you have now told *me*; but that which they told you *not*, is this— *Your* father dishonoured mine."

" 'Tis false !" exclaimed Gemma, her beautiful countenance agitated with passion."

" Let me pay the highest penalty of falsehood," said Pascal, " if it be not the truth. My mother was as virtuous as she was beautiful. The Count, your father, persecuted her with his professions of love ; she alike resisted his protestations and his threats. One day, when her loved husband was absent, she was seized by four of your father's menials, and carried by force to a country-house of his, and there by force"——

"Well, sir," said the infuriated Gemma, "the Count, my father, was Lord and master of Bauso; its inhabitants were his serfs; all they held was his. It was an honour for your mother to be noticed by such a man."

"My father," said Pascal, "thought otherwise—perhaps because he happened to be born on the estate of Prince Mocada Paterna. Let that pass,—*my* father stabbed *yours*; the wound was not mortal; for years and years I regretted that it was not; now, shame upon my weakness! I rejoice at it."

"If I recollect rightly," said Gemma, "when your father was executed as a murderer, your uncles were condemned to the galleys."

"You are correct," said Pascal, unmoved by the countess's violence; "they gave shelter to the assassin when the officers came to apprehend him; they were therefore condemned by the laws as accomplices. One was sent to Fariguana, another to Lipari, and the third to Vulcano. As for me, I was seized too, but being so young they restored me to my mother."

"And where is she?" asked Gemma, with a feeling of interest hardly definable to herself.

"She is dead," said Pascal.

"Where did she die?" asked Gemma.

"On the mountains between Pizzo di Goto and Nisi."

"She left Bauso then?" asked Gemma.

"Yes," said Pascal, "we could not bear to live there any longer. Whenever we passed the castle our eyes were

shocked with the sight of the head—the
head of *her* husband, *my* father—exposed
to public view; that was too much. She
died without a physician, without a
priest. She lies in unhallowed ground.
I—I, her only mourner, dug her grave.
Then it was," said Pascal, "as I knelt on
the fresh-turned sod, I swore before
Heaven that I, the last survivor of my
race, would avenge the wrongs of my
parents on *you*, the last of the tyrant's
family by whom we had been crushed;
but I loved Teresa. I left the hills, that
I might no longer see the grave—mute
witness of my present perjury. I bent my
steps again towards Bauso; there it was I
heard that Teresa was still here. When
the thought occurred to me of entering the Prince's service, my heart re-
volted; but love is omnipotent; my devotion to my betrothed wife has overcome

all other feelings, and here I am, a suppliant for the bounty of one whom I ought never to have approached but as a deadly foe."

" But," said Gemma, controlling the violence into which she had been betrayed, " it must be evident to you that circumstances such as your father's execution and the expatriation of your uncles must present an insurmountable obstacle to your admission into the Prince's household."

" And why?" said Pascal, " if *he* that seeks admission is willing himself to forget how all this disgrace arose."

"You must be mad to imagine the possibility of such a thing," said the countess.

" Madam," said Pascal, firmly, " you know how sacred an oath is to a mountaineer. I tell you I have one, registered in heaven. I am ready to forget it—to forget all. Revenge is sweet; do not, therefore, force me to remember."

" And if I should?" said Gemma.

" I will not think of what *might* happen," said Pascal.

" It will merely be necessary," said the countess with an air of dignity, " to take precautions, which—

" Nay," interrupted Pascal, " have mercy ; my heart's struggle is to remain honest, virtuous, and humane. Once married to Teresa, and engaged to the Prince, I could pledge myself to a life of happiness and peace ; if this must not be, I shall not return to Bauso, but—

" It is impossible," said Gemma, " that I can be your advocate."

" And yet," said Pascal, " *you* love."

The countess smiled scornfully.

" Yes, you love," continued Pascal, " and, therefore, know the force of jealousy—how its victims writhe beneath its tortures, till they grow mad. I adore Teresa—I am jealous of her, and if she is married to another I shall lose my reason, and then —"

" And then—?" repeated . Gemma, alarmed at his earnestness.

" Then !—tremble, lest there should crowd into my memory the galleys where my uncles languish, the scaffold where my father died, the unconsecrated grave where my poor mother sleeps. Countess, I say, beware !"

At this moment a cry, evidently a signal, was heard immediately under

D

the window, and, almost at the same instant, the loud ringing of a bell.

"It is the prince!" exclaimed Gemma, in a tone of assured security.

"Yes, yes, I know that," murmured Pascal; "and, before he can reach this room, you have time to pronounce the monosyllable, YES. I implore you, say the word, restore me my loved Teresa; place me in the household of his excellency, and let us be your faithful servants."

"Let me pass," said Gemma, haughtily, advancing towards the entrance of the room. Pascal, instead of showing the slightest disposition to obey her almost regal mandate, rushed before her to the door, and bolted it.

"Dare you detain me, sir?" said Gemma, seizing the bell, and crying loudly for help.

" Make no noise, madam," said Pascal, " I have said that I will do you no harm."

A second signal-cry, like the first, was heard beneath the window.

" Right, right, Ali, my child," whispered Pascal; " thou watchest faithfully. I hear the prince's step in the corridor. Madam," added he, turning to the countess; " I charge you listen to me! A moment still remains, in which you may prevent a host of evils, none of which you can anticipate as I do! One second more, and you will be too late!"

" Help, help, Rodolfo!" screamed the countess.

" You have neither heart, nor soul, nor pity—neither for others nor yourself!" cried Pascal, catching her by the hair, and stayed only from some fearful act of violence by a loud rattling at the door.

" Help !" cried Gemma, gaining confidence from the approach of assistance. " Help ! I am the prisoner of a man who threatens my life !"

" I threaten not," said Pascal, " I still entreat ; but if it must be so"——

Pascal seized the countess as a tiger would seize his prey ; being unarmed his object was to strangle her; he caught her in his arms ; a small door, at the extremity of the alcove, in which the bed stood, was suddenly opened, a pistol was fired, the room was filled with smoke, and Gemma fainted. When she recovered she found herself in the arms of the prince.

" Where is he ?" sighed she, gazing round in dread and apprehension.

" I know not," replied Carini, " I

fancy I must have missed him ; for, as I was endeavouring to get round the bed, he leaped from the window ; and, seeing you insensible, I cared for nothing else but to assure myself of your safety. And yet I see no mark of the ball in the hangings."

"Let him be pursued—captured—killed !" said Gemma ; " show him no mercy—he would have murdered me—till he is secured I cannot rest."

A search was immediately commenced, and continued all night. The town, the neighbouring gardens, the sea-beach, were all explored, but Pascal Bruno was not to be found. In the morning, drops of blood were traced from beneath the window, whence he had jumped, down to the edge of the sea.—There the clue was lost.

CHAPTER II.

WITH the first dawn of the succeeding day, the boats of the industrious fishermen were seen leaving the port and spreading themselves over the smooth surface of the bright blue sea. One of this gay and dazzling fleet, in which were a man and boy only, mixed not with the rest, but while yet in sight of Palermo, struck her sail and lay to, in a place by no means favourable for fishing.

Such a display of idleness or inactivity, might have excited some suspicions in the minds of those who were on the shore, watching the movements of the squadron, but as the boy appeared busily employed in mending nets, they thought some accident had occurred, which was probably the cause of its lingering so far behind the others.

The man was lying at the bottom of the boat, his head resting upon one of the thwarts, apparently absorbed in thought, but not so entirely abstracted, as to be prevented from mechanically scooping up some sea-water with his right hand, and bathing with it, his left shoulder, which was bound by a blood-stained bandage ; his mouth sometimes moved with a mingled expression, the real character of which, it would have been difficult to decide upon. This was Pascal Bruno.

The boy was he, who, while watching the night before under the countess's window, had twice given the signal of danger to his master. A cursory glance at this lad would have decided his origin. He was a native of the African coast, and had become the companion of Pascal under the following circumstances :

About a year previous to the period of which we are now treating, some Algerine pirates having obtained information that the Prince Moncada Paterna, a wealthy nobleman, would return from Pantelleria to Catania, in a small speronare, with not more than a dozen of his suite, concealed themselves in their vessels behind the Isle of Porri, which lies about two miles from the coast ;

perfectly aware that the prince's boat must inevitably pass through the channel, between the island and the main land. Their design was, the moment the speronare entered the strait, to dart from the little creek in which they were concealed, and surround her. The prince, however, perceiving their intentions, altered his course immediately, and bore up for the main land, hoping to get on shore at Fugallo.

The attempt was made, but in vain—in running in, the speronare grounded in three feet water. Finding themselves closely pursued, the prince and his attendants leaped into the sea, holding their firearms above their heads to keep them dry; trusting, however, to be able to reach the village, which lies about half a league inland, without being driven to the necessity of using them.

Scarcely had they reached the shore, before another party of pirates, who were lying in ambush among the reeds, rushed from their hiding-place and checked the prince's advance. Aware of the difficulty of his position, the prince and his party pushed forward, and engaged the pirates in their front; but the contest was too unequal to last long, for the party from the boats having joined their companions on the shore, further resistance was useless, and the prince surrendered, having agreed to pay ransom for his liberty, and that of his attendants, on condition of their lives being spared.

Just at the moment in which the treaty was concluded, a large body of armed peasants were seen running from the village to the scene of action. The pirates, who had attained their object by getting possession of the person of the prince, were by no means disposed to await the further advance and attack of the peasantry, and accordingly they fled to their boats with such rapidity, and in such confusion, that they left behind them three of their companions, whom they believed to be either dead or mortally wounded.

Amongst the peasants who had thus gallantly come to the rescue was Pascal Bruno, whose habits had been rendered irregular by his misfortunes, and whose disposition, unsettled by his reflections upon past events, had led him to various places since the death of his mother, and involved him in all kinds of adventurous enterprises.

When Bruno and the peasants reached the spot where the rencontre had taken place, they found one of the prince's attendants dead, and another slightly wounded. Three of the pirates were stretched on the earth, weltering in their blood—they scarcely breathed, and the savage humanity of the peasantry speedily put a period to the sufferings of two of them, with a couple of musket-balls; the third would have been in a few minutes more, relieved from all mortal misery by a pistol-bullet, had not Pascal Bruno, beholding that the intended sacrifice to mingled justice and mercy was but a child, stayed the arm just raised to decide his doom, and declared that if they would spare the boy's life he would take him under his protection.

This unlooked-for display of compassion, excited something like dissatisfaction amongst his companions, but they knew enough of Pascal Bruno to know, that what he said, was law, and that what he threatened he never hesitated to execute. Pascal seeing the ill disposition of his associates, raised his carbine, and swore that the man who lifted his finger against the boy, should have its contents through his head. Bold and unmanageable as a crowd may be, whenever it appears that any one life is to be hazarded by the attainment of the particular object desired by all, that object is generally abandoned in the readiest manner; no individual choosing, knowingly, to doom himself to the death which may be his lot for the benefit of the community at large. The peasants looked at Pascal, then at the boy, and then at each other, and the result of these various observations was, that they permitted Pascal Bruno to take his foundling in his arms, and carry him away; and not a murmur of discontent was heard at his doing so.

Bruno conveyed his prize to the boat in which he was constantly sailing from one point to another, scarce resting at any, and in managing which, he was so skilful, that she seemed to obey him with the readiness of a horse long and well accustomed to its rider. Once on board, he hoisted his sail, and steered towards the Cape of Aliga Grande.

As soon as he found that the boat held her course and required no pilot, he lashed her helm, and turned his attention to the wounded boy, who still remained insensible. He gently removed the white Bournous in which the little fellow was enveloped, and untied the girdle to which still hung his ataghan. By the last rays of the setting sun, he discovered that he had been seriously wounded; a bullet had struck him between the right shoulder and the ribs, and had passed out very near the spine.

Bruno carefully bathed the wound, and the refreshing sensation caused by the application of the water, and the balmy influence of the evening breeze, excited symptoms of returning animation and consciousness in the child; for although he did not unclose his eyes, his lips moved, and he muttered some unintelligible words. Bruno aware of the fever, which a shot, such as the poor boy had received must naturally induce, put a flask of fresh water to his lips—he drank eagerly—again tried to speak, and relapsed into a swoon. Pascal laid him as gently as possible at the bottom of the boat, and kept continually bathing his wound, with a cloth which he kept moist

by dipping it in the sea, the briny qua-
lities of which, are in great repute
amongst the sailors in the Mediterranean,
for their healing tendency.

It was just about the time of vespers,
when our voyagers found themselves off
the harbour of Ragusa. The wind was
fair, and Pascal found little difficulty in
getting into the river, and in three hours,
leaving Modica to the right, he passed
the bridge which crosses the road from
Nola to Chiaromonte. The river is not
navigable, for more than half a league
beyond this, and when he could proceed
no farther, he dragged his boat ashore,
among the tufts of laurels, roses, and
papyrus, which fringe its verdant
banks.

Again he lifted the boy in his arms and
traversed the country with his burden. It
was not long before he reached the

opening of a valley, into which he descended, and pursued his way until he discovered on his right an abrupt, perpendicular hill, the wall-like face of which exhibited at intervals marks of excavations, which in other days served as retreats for the Troglodytes, the first inhabitants of the island, to whom the eventual civilization of the Greek colonies is ascribed.

Pascal entered one of these caverns, which communicated by steps with an upper apartment, into which a square hole, by way of window, admitted the air : a bed of rushes lay in one corner, over which he spread the boy's shawl, and laid him upon it. Having descended and lit a fire, he speedily returned with a lighted brand, which he stuck into the wall, and then seated himself on a stone

E

near the bed, anxiously awaiting his young patient's restoration to consciousness.

This was not the first visit Bruno had made to that retreat. In the vague rambles and fruitless expeditions over the island, by which he hoped to calm his restless spirit, beguile his solitary hours, and lead his mind from evil thoughts by which it was sometimes occupied, he had explored this valley, and occupied that very chamber dug in the rock three thousand years before. There it was that he had abandoned himself to reflections which, groundless and incoherent as they were, are natural to all men whose heated imaginations are uncontrolled by education. He knew that a race now gone from the face of the earth had in far distant ages dug these caves, and deeply imbued with a superstition too general amongst his countrymen, believed, in common with all the neighbouring inhabitants, that their first tenants were magicians and enchanters. This belief, far from operating with him as it did upon the weaker intellects of the surrounding peasantry, by keeping them away from these awful precincts, insensibly and unconsciously attracted him to their solemn solitude. In his childhood he had heard of charmed rifles, of men rendered invulnerable by magic, of travellers invisible by mortal eye, and the sole hope and object of his fearless, wonder-loving mind, was to encounter some mysterious being—some sorcerer —some demon even, who, in barter for his soul's peace, would invest him with superhuman attributes, which might render him superior to the rest of mankind.

But it was in vain that he invoked the spirits of the long-departed inhabitants of the valley of Modica. No sign nor token did he receive to encourage his hopes ; no apparition answered to his supplications ; and Pascal Bruno, to his serious disappointment, remained a man like other men, except, indeed, that he was far superior in courage and address to the generality of the race of mountaineers to which he now belonged.

For nearly an hour had Pascal been absorbed in one of his stormy day-dreams, when the wounded boy appeared to wake from the sort of lethargy in which he so long had slumbered—he opened his eyes, looked wildly round, and then gazed intently upon his deliverer, ignorant, as yet, whether he beheld in him a friend or a foe.

Natural instinct led his hand to the hilt of his trusty ataghan—it was gone—he heaved a deep sigh, and his head again sank on its rude pillow.

Pascal was aware that the Lingua-Franca is universally understood on the shores of the Mediterranean, from Marseilles to Alexandria, and from Constantinople to Algiers; in fact it is generally available all over the continent of the Old World. It was in this language Pascal softly inquired of the boy if he suffered much.

" Who asks that question?" said the boy.

" A friend," replied Pascal.

" Then I am not a prisoner?" said the boy.

"No."

"How, then, came I here?"

Pascal related to him all the circumstances of the affair which had thrown him into his present position. He listened attentively to the history with his eyes fixed upon the narrator, and when he ceased to speak, exclaimed, in a tone of the deepest gratitude,

"Then as you have saved my life you will be a father to me?"

"I will," said Bruno.

"Father," said the boy, "your son is called Ali—and you—"

"PASCAL BRUNO."

"Allah protect thee!" said the boy.

"Tell me, my child," said Pascal, "do you desire any thing?"

"Water is all I ask," said Ali; "for I am parched with thirst."

Pascal took an earthen cup from a small recess in the rock, and went down to fill it from a neighbouring spring; as he returned his eyes fell on the boy's ataghan—it lay where he had left it—Ali had made no effort to regain it. He caught the cup from Pascal's hand with eagerness, and quaffed its entire contents at a draught.

" May Allah grant thee as many happy years of life as there were drops of water in this cup !" said the grateful Ali.

" You are a good boy, Ali," muttered Bruno, whose stern heart, full of a thousand pangs and bitternesses, melted at the poor child's prayer. " Make haste, my boy, and get well; and when you have sufficiently recovered you shall, if you wish it, return to Africa.

The boy did recover, and yet he returned not to Africa. He remained in Sicily with Bruno, to whom he became so fondly and faithfully attached, that he could not endure the thoughts of their separation. From the hour in which Ali was able to resume his activity, he and his new father were never apart—he was his companion on the mountains; shooting; or sailing on the sea; hunting up his game, or helping to navigate his boat—ever constant and ready, as he had declared, to lay down his life for his preserver.

He it was, who, on the evening when Pascal paid his unwelcome and unexpected visit to the villa of Prince Carini, watched under the window during his father's interview with Gemma. It was he who gave the two signals beneath the balcony;—the first, when the prince rang at the gate; the second, when he saw him enter the house—Ali was himself on the point of climbing to the window to succour his father, if aid were wanted, when he saw him leap to the ground. He followed him as he fled towards the sea—they reached the water's edge together—threw themselves into the boat, and, as it would have been impossible for them to sail at that period of the evening without exciting suspicion, they were obliged to satisfy themselves by mingling in the crowd of fishing-boats which waited only for the morning's dawn to take their departure.

During that anxious night Ali afforded Pascal similar assistance, to that which Pascal had bestowed upon him under similar circumstances. The prince had hit his man, and the ball, which was vainly looked for in the hangings of the apartment, had almost traversed and lodged in the fleshy part of Bruno's shoulder, so that Ali was able, unskilled even as he was in the art of surgery, to extract it on the side opposite to that by which it had entered, by making a very slight incision in the flesh with his ataghan. While this was doing, Bruno seemed scarcely to think of his hurt, or feel the pain which it could not fail to inflict. When it was done, all that he did towards healing the wound was to bathe it constantly with sea-water, while Ali continued to appear as if he were busily employed in mending their nets.

"Father," said Ali, suddenly leaving off his pretended work, " turn round and look towards the shore."

"What's there, child?" said Pascal.

"A crowd of people," replied the boy.

"Point out," said Pascal, "in which direction."

"There," replied Ali, "below, on the road that leads to the church."

So it was. A considerable number of persons were moving up the road which winds round the holy mountain. Pascal immediately recognised it as a bridal procession, on its way to the chapel of St. Rosalia.

"Get the boat's head to the shore, Ali," cried Pascal, "and row with all your strength."

The boy seized an oar with each hand, and pulled his best. The little vessel seemed to fly along the surface of the water. The nearer they approached the land, the more agitated became the countenance of Bruno. When about half a mile from it, he satisfied himself of the correctness of his almost intuitive suspicion that it was his affianced wife then actually on her way to the altar with his successful rival, Gaetano.

" It is Teresa !" exclaimed he. " They have hurried on this wedding—it was not to have been till Sunday—but they did not venture to wait till then, lest, between this day and that, I should carry her off. Well! Heaven is my witness I have done all in my power to make this affair terminate happily. It is the fault of others it has ended thus—on *their* heads be the punishment."

Having gazed on the scene before him for a few minutes, during which it was evident to Ali that thoughts of deep

revenge were occupying his mind, he
directed the boy to cease rowing, and to
hoist the sail ; then, without saying one
word more upon the subject of what he had
just witnessed, he put the boat before the
wind, and in less than two hours she
disappeared behind Cape Gallo. The
course of proceeding adopted by Pascal
towards the destroyers of his happiness,
will be detailed in the next chapter.

CHAPTER III.

PASCAL was right in his conjectures, as to the premature celebration of the nuptials. The countess, not without reason, as we have seen, apprehending some desperate attempt on the part of Bruno, accelerated the marriage of Teresa, three days ; but, alas, without telling her that Bruno had been in Palermo, and that he still loved her devotedly, and that for her sake he had overcome his aversion from entering the

service of the prince, or indeed mentioning to her, that she had seen and con-
versed with him. Teresa, therefore, wholly
unconscious of the deep interest which
her first lover still retained for her; un-
aware of the sacrifice which he was ready
to make for her, and implicitly confiding
in the mistress, who, with all her sins upon
her head, had taught her to love her,
offered no opposition to the new arrangement; and as Gaetano and herself, from
feelings of peculiar piety and devotion,
desired to be married at the chapel of
St. Rosalia, the patroness of Palermo,
the countess, too anxious to have the affair
concluded as speedily as possible, con-
sented to the arrangement, and there
accordingly they were married.

In England, a wedding is an April-like
ceremony, an affair of mingled smiles
and tears, in which the latter generally

predominate.   There were no tears shed
at Teresa's nuptials, but still there hung
over the brightness of her future prospects
in the service of the countess, a wild dark
cloud, which seemed to take the form of
her loved, lost Pascal; nor could she
dispel the vision which she dreaded to
look on. The ceremony, however, was performed, and after its conclusion the wedding party descended to Palermo, where
carriages were in waiting, to convey the
company to the village of Carini, from which
"ten acres of territory," the prince derived
his title.   There, by order of the liberal
countess (for ladies of the countess's character, are uniformly liberal in matters of
festivity and gaiety), a splendid fête was
prepared; all the country people from
the surrounding villages had been invited, and flocked from Montreal, Capaci,
Favarotta, and other places, three or

four leagues distant ; and amongst all the girls who were playing off their coquettish tricks, those of Piana de Greci, were particularly distinguished by their punctilious adherence to what they call their national costume, although the people from whom it was actually derived, had left the land of their birth for other countries, twelve hundred years before the new-comers settled there.

Tables had been laid along an esplanade shaded by verdant oaks and spreading pines, to which the gentle breeze wafted the luscious perfume of the orange and the citron. Around the "shady blest retreat," flourished in all their rich luxuriance, the fig and pomegranate a double blessing from Providence, which " kindly bounteous, cares for all," and commiserating at once the hunger

F

and thirst of the Sicilian poor, scatters these fruitful trees like manna over the grateful land. This esplanade was approached by a walk, bordered with aloes, whose towering stems looked from afar like the bright lances of Arab horsemen, and, although the view towards the south, was bounded by the palace itself, the lofty chain of mountains which divide the island into its three principal districts, were seen towering above its terraces.   At the extremity of each valley, the lovely Sicilian sea caught the eye, which from the bright variety of its tints, might have been mistaken for three distinct seas ; since from the effect produced by the rays of the sun, which was fast sinking in the horizon towards Palermo, it was in one part of a deep blue tint, while in another, its waves were silvery bright, even while its billows dashing against the rocks of St. Vito, looked like liquid gold.

As soon as the dessert was put down, and when the nuptial festivity was at its height, the doors of the palace were thrown open, and Gemma, leaning on the prince's arm, preceded by servants bearing torches, and followed by their suite, descended the steps of the terrace, and proceeded to the banquet. The country-people were rising from their seats, when the prince motioned to them not to disturb themselves, and with Gemma still leaning on his arm, his Excellency began a tour round the tables; and concluded the " progress," by stopping before the newly-married couple. A servant took a golden cup to Gaetano, who filling it with wine, presented it to

Gemma. The beautiful countess wishing the bride and bridegroom joy, touched the brim with her ruby lips, and handed the cup to the prince, who drank off its contents, and threw into it a purse of gold, which was carried to Teresa, as her wedding present.

Shouts instantly arose of "Long live the Prince of Carini!" "Long live the Countess of Castel-Nuovo!" The esplanade was at this moment suddenly illuminated, as if by magic, in the midst of which the illustrious visiters withdrew, leaving behind them the light and joy of some bright vision, which had too quickly faded.

These noble personages had scarcely entered the castle with their attendants before music was heard; the young folks left the tables, and hurried to the place

allotted for dancing. Gaetano, according
to the established Sicilian custom in such
matters, prepared to open the ball with
the interesting Teresa, whose beauty and
grace of manner, had been the subject
of general admiration throughout the
day. He approached her with the finished
air of third-rate gracefulness—a sort of
lively caricature of the best Sicilian
cavaliers, and in the highest possible
spirits, solicited the honour of her hand.
At that moment, a stranger presented
himself on the esplanade, and stood in
the midst of the company gazing upon
the scene. The looks of the whole
assembly were turned towards the new
comer, who was dressed in the Calabrian
costume, wearing pistols and a dagger
in his belt; his jacket slung over one
shoulder, like an hussar's pelisse, left
open to view his other sleeve stained

with blood. Teresa saw him—she gazed on him for a moment—uttered a faint cry, and remained pale and motionless, as if she had seen a spectre.

It was PASCAL BRUNO.

Every eye was fixed on the uninvited guest; a dead and awful silence reigned. Every one present felt assured of the approach of some terrible catastrophe.

Pascal, apparently unmoved by the sensation he had created, walked directly up to Teresa, and standing before her, folded his arms, and fixed his piercing eyes on her pale countenance.

" Pascal," said Teresa, in a faltering voice, " Pascal, can it be *you?*"

" Yes, Teresa," said Bruno, in a deep hollow voice, " it is I. I heard at Bauso, where I patiently and confidently waited your return, that you were to be married at Carini; so I came hither, and I hope am in time to dance the first Tarantella with you."

"I beg your pardon, sir," said Gaetano, coming up to him with a mingled air of anger and of gaiety, " that is the bridegroom's right."

" It is the right of the affianced one," said Pascal. " Come, my beloved Teresa, this is the least you can do for me after all I have suffered for *you*."

" Teresa is *my* wife," said Gaetano, stretching forth his arm toward him.

" Teresa is *my* betrothed," said Pascal, taking her hand.

" Help! oh, help !" said the wretched girl.

The appeal was irresistible—the effect instantaneous. Gaetano seized Bruno by the collar — they struggled for a moment—that was all—in another instant

Gaetano uttered a piercing cry, and fell
dead at his feet.   Pascal's dagger was
buried to the hilt in his breast.   Some of
the men, who were nearest him on the
instant rushed towards the murderer to
secure him.   Bruno stood unmoved, and
drawing one of his pistols from his belt,
waved it over his head as a signal to the
musicians, to strike up the Tarantella.
They obeyed as it were mechanically.
The rest of the company, paralyzed by
the suddenness and fearfulness of what
had happened, remained motionless.

" Come, Teresa, come, let us begin,"
said Pascal.

Teresa was no longer in possession of
her faculties, she had become a creature
demented by fear.   She unconsciously
yielded to his guidance, and this horrible
dance, close to the corpse of the in-

offensive murdered young man, was continued by the musicians to the last strain. Incredible as it may appear, no one stirred—no one spoke—it was something too terrific—something so unnaturally horrid that nature itself seemed palsied. The moment the music ceased, as if it had been all that had excited and sustained her, the wretched Teresa fell fainting on the body of Gaetano.

" Thanks, Teresa," said Pascal, " that is all I wanted; and now, if any man wishes to know me *here*, that he may find me *elsewhere*, I am PASCAL BRUNO."

" The son of Antonio," ventured one voice, " whose head is exposed to public view at the castle of Bauso ?"

" The same," said Pascal; " but if you wish to see that sight again, you had better make good speed. I promise you, whomsoever you may be, it shall not be there long."

Saying which Pascal disappeared ; and, amongst the many who were bidden to the wedding-feast, not one of the guests felt the slightest desire, or exhibited the least inclination to follow him ; they all anxiously, considerately no doubt, and certainly most naturally, turned their thoughts and attentions to Gaetano and Teresa.

The one was dead, the other senseless.

That a tragedy, so revolting as this, could have been acted with impunity seems almost impossible. It never *could* have been, had Prince Carini been on the spot. He and the countess, however, had returned to Palermo directly after they quitted the gardens, and it was not until the following morning that they were made acquainted with the horrid business. The humble guests were paralyzed by the appearance and savage resolution of Pascal, and individual apprehension in every one of them, similar to that which upon another occasion gave Bruno possession of Ali, practically proved the power of a single death-dealing weapon over a herd of unarmed peasants.

In the morning every means was adopted, by order of the prince, to apprehend the murderer, but in vain; he had escaped, leaving an impression of dread and apprehension for the future, upon the mind of Gemma, which not all the consolation and assurances of the prince could alleviate or mitigate. This natural solicitude for her own personal safety was rendered more galling by the consciousness that she was, in fact, herself the primary cause of the disaster. The selfishness which led her to retain Teresa and reject her affianced lover, and the duplicity to which, in order to secure the object which she considered essential to her comfort, she had descended, in not communicating to the unfortunate girl the fact of Pascal's unchanged and unwearied affection, and the resolution to which he had come for *her* sake, added to the reflection that she herself had hurried on the wedding so sadly celebrated, overwhelmed her with grief and sorrow.

Pascal, however, was still at liberty, and stirring in the cause of vengeance; again he visited his mother's grave—; again and again kissed the turf with which he had covered her remains, and, kneeling on the spot where he had sworn the bitter oath which love had induced him to retract, renewed his vow, satisfied that nothing now was left for him on earth which could tempt him again to violate it.

The Sunday following the fatal marriage, the day indeed on which it was to have been celebrated according to the countess's first arrangement, was the fête-day at Bauso. Never did village present a gayer aspect, all the inhabitants were enjoying themselves; some drinking in the cabarets, others dancing and singing in the streets, which were filled with light hearts and merry faces, especially that which led up to the castle, which was absolutely crowded with people pressing forward to see the young men of the neighbourhood shoot at a mark. The

prize to be contended for was a silver
cup, to be purchased with the contribu-
tions of those who proposed to try their
skill. Any one so inclined deposited two
carlins for each shot he intended to have;
upon the payment of which moderate
sum, he received a card, drawn at random,
the number written upon which, was to
decide the order of firing. Indifferent
shots took ten, twelve, or fourteen of
these chances; men more confident of
their skill took four or five; but in the
midst of the struggle for cards upon the
present occasion one hand was extended
to deposit the required two carlins, and
to receive in exchange but one ticket.
The eyes of the rival candidates for
the cup were turned with more surprise
than pleasure upon a person who thus
either practically evinced so much self-

confidence, or whose circumstances would not permit him to venture his money to any greater extent.

The rival who had thus excited their apprehensions and their curiosity, was a tall powerful man, enveloped in a large cloak, which covered all the lower part of his face ; his hat was studiously drawn down over his forehead, but did not fall sufficiently low to conceal a pair of piercing black eyes ; he drew his card ; the other aspirants were in due time all supplied, and they forthwith proceeded to the shooting-ground.

The place appointed for this trial of skill was an open space in front of the castle, and the mark was placed directly under the iron cage, in which the head of Antonio Bruno was exposed to view. This cage as it was called, like all cages used for a similar purpose in Italy, had no bars in the front, but could only be reached by a staircase in the interior of the castle, leading to a window, on the outside of which, the back of the cage was fastened. The people of Bauso so long accustomed to behold this appalling object, were no longer affected by the sight of it, and fortunate it was, that habit had so familiarized them with it; for having been purposely fixed, in what might be considered the *Place* of their village, the very centre of every fête, or fair, or public reunion, which might take place, it was constantly before their eyes, in the midst of their greatest gaieties.

The shooting began—every shot was greeted by the spectators with applause, or laughter proportionate to its merits;

but after a short time, and when several of the balls had struck near the centre of the target, the affair acquired a deeper interest, and the noise of the bystanders had subsided into silent anxiety.

The stranger still enveloped in his cloak, seemed not to enter into the feelings of those about him ; he stood leaning on his English rifle, his eyes fixed upon the ground, waiting his turn to fire—it came—his number was called—he looked round apparently unconscious that it was his ; but recovering himself, after a moment's pause, he advanced to the cord which was stretched across the ground to mark the spot from whence he was to fire—all eyes were on him—some fancied they knew him — others proclaimed him to be a stranger—there was something mysterious and mystifying

G

about him, and the interest he excited was universal.

He levelled his rifle carefully and deliberately — took his aim low, and raised the barrel slowly and steadily— The whole assembly were earnestly watching him. It was with immeasurable surprise they beheld him still raising the rifle, even above the line of the target, till he covered the fatal cage—for a second, the stranger paused, as if his arm had been paralyzed—he fired—the ball had done its duty — the head of Antonio Bruno rolled from its degrading receptacle, and fell at the foot of the target—a thrill of horror pervaded the whole crowd — a mute silence ensued—no shout of approbation followed the successful shot. The stranger stepped forward and lifted the livid object from the ground — he enveloped it in the ample folds of his cloak, which falling from his shoulders exhibited to the inhabitants of Bauso, the figure of PASCAL BRUNO.

"So far am I revenged!" exclaimed he, in a tone of agonized feeling ; "but let no man follow me."

Laden with his dreadful burden, Pascal without saying one syllable more, or even looking once behind him, struck into the path which leads from the village to the mountains.

The effect produced by this event upon the inhabitants, was at the moment, terrific and appalling ; but there was no disposition evinced to deprive him of the horrid prize he had gained. The fate of Antonio Bruno was discussed by the people of the village in very different terms from those used by the family of

Castel-Nuovo. He had been an honest and much-esteemed man, a fond father, and an affectionate husband. He that doomed him to die, had been his oppressor and betrayer : and even if justice demanded as the price of his attempt on the count's life, under circumstances the most aggravating and heart-rending, that he should suffer death, and that his head should remain exposed, in the very village of which he was once a respected inhabitant ; now that justice had been satisfied, and that the castle of Bauso had, upon the death of his prosecutor, passed out of his family, it seemed cruel over-much to continue the horrid exhibition. This was the general feeling amongst the inhabitants, although none dare make it known to the present possessor of the domain ; therefore no man stepped forward to stop Pascal's passage ; he had done that which in fact was grateful to them, and knowing but little of the secret springs of his actions, they speedily dispersed, and went to their homes, praising the filial devotion and gallant conduct of PASCAL BRUNO.

CHAPTER IV.

WE have already stated that Prince Carini, the moment he was made acquainted with the extraordinary murder of Gaetano, put in motion all the resources of which he had the command, in order to ensure the apprehension of Pascal Bruno. The task was one which involved much difficulty, and the mingled boldness and dexterity of the culprit promised (to use a sporting phrase) much sport to the commandants of companies, and their agents, in effecting the capture. They were, however, indefatigable in their exertions, and one morning intelligence was brought to the principal magistrate at Spadafora, that Pascal had passed through that village during the preceding night on his road to Divieto. The moment this important news reached the said functionary, he took all necessary measures to secure the assassin, fully convinced that he would take advantage of the darkness of the following night to return by the same route.

In compliance with the demand of the magistrate a military force was put at his disposal, and a party of soldiers were placed in ambush on the road-side, for the purpose of intercepting Pascal as he re-.

traced his steps from Divieto. During the whole of the night they carefully observed, and even challenged, every person travelling in that direction; but no Pascal Bruno appeared. In the daytime they were withdrawn from their concealment, but on the following night they again took up their position, again waited and watched, and again were disappointed.

On the third morning, which was *the* Sunday, quite sufficiently fatigued with their two nights' vigilant inspection of passengers on the road, the soldiers gladly proceeded to a small inn, not more than twenty paces from the highway, to breakfast; but just before the meal, for which their night duty had so admirably sharpened their appetites, was served, and while they were yet regaling their noses with the savoury fumes of the repast which they so anxiously anticipated, the magistrate's clerk rushed into the room where they were awaiting the appearance of their host with all the comestibles—(or as a respectable lady of our acquaintance, long since gathered to her fathers or mothers, called them, combustibles)—and announced that Pascal Bruno was quietly descending the mountain from the Divieto side.

Although the soldiers were as brave as lions, and were, moreover, in a majority of twenty to one against Pascal Bruno on the present occasion, the tocsin sounded by the tongue of their informant seemed infinitely less harmonious at that moment than it might have been if it had been heard after breakfast. However, there was no alternative, duty must be done; and having armed themselves they turned out in "double quick" in order to capture the object of their pursuit. As for their ambuscade that could not be reached in time, for Pascal was within a hundred yards of them; under which circumstance, as discretion is the better part of valour, and stratagem sometimes succeeds where open opposition would fail, the gallant corps drew up in front of the inn, but in a quiet and unmilitary manner, in order that Bruno might not imagine that they had any hostile intentions towards him, but, on the contrary, to induce him to believe them a party of agreeable persons coming forth to take the air after their morning meal.

The bird they had flushed, however, was somewhat too old and wary to be so

caught. His first glance at these distinguished and stratagetical heroes convinced him of their real business and intentions, as far as regarded himself; nevertheless, instead of wheeling round and
cantering away from them, he put spurs to
his horse and dashed along the road at a
gallop. Still concealing their object,
and reserving their fire until he should be
within the certain reach of their carbines,
the moment he passed in front of them
the whole party saluted him with a volley:
the balls struck up the dust at his horse's
feet, a cloud of smoke enveloped Pascal,
but horse and rider pursued the "even
tenour of their way" unhurt. The officer
looked at the soldiers; the soldiers
looked at the officer; and then they all
looked at each other :—a picked party of

riflemen to have missed an object within thirty paces of them—what could it mean? The thing *had* happened, and the game was up: all that the officer could do was to report to the magistrate what had occurred.

The account of this escape reached Bauso the same evening, which, coupled with what they had themselves seen of the shooting in the earlier part of that day, excited a powerful suspicion amongst the inhabitants that Pascal bore a charmed life; which suspicion was strengthened into an implicit belief by the fact, that on the following morning the jacket which he had worn the previous day was found hooked upon the doorpost of the house of the judge at Bauso, perforated by thirteen shots, and in its pockets were found the thirteen bullets which had pierced the cloth, flattened into the shape of so many carlins.

Some of the long-headed people of Bauso, and who, besides being too religious to believe in mysterious agencies, were not disposed to assign such attributes of superhuman superiority to Pascal, suggested that he might have hung his jacket upon a tree, and have fired these thirteen bullets at it, himself, as a man sometimes ventures to fire one at a friend, for the sake of making a reputation; but certain it is that the majority of the people of Bauso set him down for possessing an unearthly power over his fellow-creatures.

In colder climates than that of Sicily the snowball gathers much in rolling; and in all climates, hot or cold, a story gains a vast deal by frequent repetition : the moment these histories got wind, it was wonderful to see how their character rose and their importance increased. The weakest are naturally the most credulous, and as the weakest are by far the most numerous class of society, the rapidity and extent of circulation of such matters is easily accounted for. In less than three months after his miraculous escape, it was generally reported that one night, during a storm which shook the whole island to its centre, Pascal had entered into a dreadful league with a sorceress, and had succeeded in his long-cherished wish of bartering his soul in exchange for the power of transporting himself, in the twinkling of an eye, from one end of Sicily to the other —invisibly, if he chose ; but, if not, safe from the effects of fire, sword, and bullet. This compact, they said, was to last for three years and no longer; that period having been in Pascal's estimation sufficient for the consummation of his just vengeance.

As to Pascal himself, far from undeceiving the people of Bauso upon these points, his object was to corroborate all their suspicions and substantiate all their surmises, which exertions of his own, coupled with the circumstances already narrated, perfectly succeeded in forming for him the character which he had so long and so ardently desired. One strong proof of the potency of the imaginary spell by which he was supposed to be protected is, that after his escape and the exhibition of his jacket, not a man could be found who would undertake even to attempt his capture for the murder of Gaetano.

In less than a year from the period of Gaetano's death, all Sicily rang with the extraordinary exploits of Pascal Bruno ——the invulnerable, inexplicable Pascal Bruno. Invulnerable he was thought to be——inexplicable he most assuredly was; for, whelmed in crime, implacable in revenge, and reckless of consequences, the conduct he observed, wherever he had power or influence, was marked by the strictest sense of honour and of justice—— conduct so incompatible with every thing he had done as regarded himself and his own particular circumstances, as perhaps to justify, in a greater degree, the suspicion entertained in Sicily of his unearthly character, than one could otherwise imagine possible. Wherever the rich oppressed the poor, wherever the strong attempted to tyrannize over the weak, there Pascal appeared, and, by

the intervention of his mountain law, or
rather equity, kept the balance even;
and this course he adopted more especially as regarded the inhabitants of
Bauso and its neighbourhood, in which,
after the deliverance of his father's head,
he had fixed his residence, and where he
alone maintained a most surprising degree of authority. It was, however, this
disposition to check the arbitrary power of
the higher orders under which, in the bit-
terness of his soul, he felt that his parents
and himself had so cruelly suffered, which
ensured his safety in the fastness he had
chosen for his retreat, which was no
other than the ruins of the fortress of
Castel-Nuovo, once the possession of
his deadliest foe. The poor and weak
counteract by their numbers the influence of the rich and strong—Pascal,

H

the champion of the more numerous
class, became their idol—they were de-
voted to his interests, and every attempt
upon his life or liberty was defeated by
their vigilance. Nay they had even con-
certed signals in order to forewarn him
of any approaching danger.

In the neighbourhood of Bauso, if a
rich landlord had demanded an excessively high rent of a poor farmer—if a
propitious marriage was about to be
broken off by the avarice of a niggard
father—if the corrupt judgment of a petty
tribunal had doomed an innocent man to
punishment — in short, if oppression or
injustice were detected, and Pascal was
informed of it, he took his carbine and
his pistols, let loose his four dogs—his
only followers—mounted his horse, and
quitting the ruins in which he had taken
up his abode, set off forthwith to reason

with the landlord, the father, or the judge, nor left him till he got an assurance that the rent should be lowered, the maiden married, or the prisoner released. It was by this sort of equitable intervention and arbitration, that the brigand, Pascal Bruno, gained the hearts of those in whose keeping his safety was placed.

Philanthropy seems a somewhat strange resident in the breast of a murderer ; but it should be recollected that the savage part of Pascal's character developed itself only when what he felt to be the personal injuries he had received, called for personal vengeance. Abstracted from the one great object of his life, his feelings were chivalrous, and, as we have already said, his heart and disposition generous. On the one point he was mad—to revenge the wrongs of his parents he had sworn—against the fulfilment of his cruel oath he suffered nothing to oppose itself, and wherever an act, however daring or however trivial, might in his opinion conduce, it mattered not how slightly, to the attainment of that one object, no law, human or divine, could stay his hand.

Upon one occasion—before he had so firmly established his extraordinary reputation with the people of Bauso—he resolved to raise two hundred ounces of gold—for what?—to better his own condition—to afford him pleasures—to procure him luxuries?—No! to rebuild the house of an honest innkeeper which had been accidentally burnt down. Money of his own he had none; he therefore determined to write to the Prince Butera to ask him for the loan of the required sum, pointing out a particular spot on the mountain where his Highness might bury it in the ground, and where his Highness's correspondent would, on a particular night, go to look for it; adding, that in case his request was not complied with, it would inevitably assume the character of a demand; and announcing that in that case open war would be declared between the Monarch of the mountain and the Lord of the valley. If, on the contrary, the favour were granted, the amount would be faithfully repaid to his Highness out of the first money that Pascal might be able to *draw* from the regal treasury.

The Prince Butera was one of those splendid examples which modern history seldom affords. He was a relic of ancient Sicilian nobility, chivalrous and bold as the Normans, from whom their order sprang. Hercules was he called, and his fine athletic figure seemed formed

upon the model of his mythological name-
sake. He could fell to the earth a restiff
horse with one blow of his fist, break
across his knee a bar of iron half an
inch thick, and bend a piaster between
his fingers.

One striking specimen of his coolness
in the midst of danger, had rendered
him extremely popular with the inhabitants of Palermo. In the year 1770,
there was a great scarcity of bread in
that city—a violent insurrection was the
consequence. The governor was compelled in self-defence, to have recourse
to the *ultima ratio ;* a cannon was planted
in the streets. The people pushed
forward towards the gun, and the artil-
lery-man who held the match was about
to fire it upon the mob, when the Prince
Butera seating himself on the mouth
of the piece as calmly and as carelessly

as if throwing himself into an arm-chair, addressed them in a speech so reasonable, and so eloquent, that the mob fell back, the cannon was withdrawn unfired, and the blood of the people was unshed. Nor was this the sole cause of the Prince's popularity.

It was his custom to walk every morning on the terrace which overlooks the Marina; and as the gates of his palace were always open to the public at daybreak, he usually found congregated about him, a very large assemblage of poor people. Upon these occasions he used to wear a buckskin leather waistcoat, the excessively roomy pockets of which, were every morning filled with carlins and half-carlins, by his valet, every one of which disappeared before his return to the palace. But his dispensations of charity, were made in a manner at once peculiar and unnatural to him, inasmuch as he outwardly appeared very much disposed to knock down every poor person who ventured to implore his benevolence; an appearance which considering his Highness's bulk and capabilities was any thing but agreeable or soothing to the mendicants.

"Prince," says a poor woman, surrounded by her infant-family, "have pity upon the poor mother of five children."

"Five children!" answers his Highness, "what are your five children to me? they are none of them mine, I suppose?" and then with a look of assumed anger, he lets fall a piece of money in her apron.

"Prince," says another, "I have had no bread to eat these two days."

"Go along you foolish fellow!" replies the Prince, feigning to give him a blow with his fist, which would have been enough to feed him for a week, "how can I help *that?* I don't make bread. Why don't you go to the baker?" affording him at the same moment, ample means to follow his advice. The consequence was, that the Prince Butera was received by the people wherever he went with every mark of affection and respect.

One person, however, complained bitterly of his Highness's liberality, and that was his Maître d'hôtel, who by no means approved of the indiscriminate admission of guests of all ranks and conditions to his illustrious master's table. The Prince's dinners were of the first order, and notwithstanding their luxury and magnificence, his Highness literally kept open house, his parties seldom consisting of less than twenty or thirty, of whom seven or eight, were generally strangers; while the greater number of those who were not, dined as regularly with his Highness, as the most punctual customers of a popular table d'hôte.

Amongst this latter class, was one Captain Altavilla, who had obtained his rank in the army, by following Cardinal Ruffo from Palermo to Naples, and who had returned from Naples to Palermo, with a pension of a thousand ducats. Unfortunately, the Captain like many of his betters was sadly addicted to play; his ill-luck at which, would have rendered his income wholly inadequate to his expenditure, had he not hit upon two plans, the execution of which rendered his quarter's pay the least important branch of his revenue.

The first of these plans was to dine every day at the Prince's table, which, as we have already seen, was no very difficult object to achieve, since it was free to all ; but the second was something a little more perilous, and not quite so venial. Every day after he *had* dined, the Captain contrived regularly to carry off the silver fork and spoon, which he had used at dinner. This very gentlemanly proceeding went on for some time without detection and even without the diurnal abstraction of the articles being discovered ; but profusely as his Highness's sideboards were furnished, the diminution of stock at length became evident to the Major-domo, and having, as servants sometimes will, taken a strong aversion from the Captain, his suspicions fell upon *him;* he began to watch his movements carefully ; two or three days only were required to convert those suspicions into certainty, and having established the fact to his entire satisfaction, the vigilant domestic proceeded forthwith to inform his illustrious master of the fact.

The Prince having heard the story, paused for a moment, and then said very quietly, " I don't know—I am very sorry for it — but as long as the Captain pockets only his own fork and spoon, I have nothing to say—when he begins to walk off with those of his neighbours, I must make up my mind to do something," and in consequence of this extraordinary show of lenity, the Captain, to the great discomfiture of the Major-domo, continued one of the constant guests at the palace of his Excellency the Prince de Butera.

The Prince was at his villa at Castrogiovanni, when Pascal Bruno's letter requesting the loan of the two hundred ounces of gold was brought to him. He read it, and asked if any body waited for an answer. Upon being told that there did not, he folded up the letter, and put it in his pocket, as if it had been any ordinary communication.

The appointed night arrived — the place in which Pascal had desired the Prince to deposit the money was on the southern acclivity of Etna, near one of the thousand extinct craters, which had derived a temporary existence, from the eternal flame of the great volcano, and which, short as that existence was, had been adequate to the destruction of the towns which were in their immediate neighbourhood. The one of which we speak, is called Montebaldo, for each of these awful hillocks 'received a name as soon as it rose from the earth.

Within ten minutes' walk from its base, stands a vast isolated tree, known as the " Chestnut of the Hundred Horses ;" because under its branches which formed a little forest of themselves, it was said one hundred mounted horsemen might be sheltered. Thither Pascal repaired to seek his required gold, which he had directed the Prince to bury at its foot. He left Cantorbi at eleven o'clock; it was near midnight when the gigantic object struck his sight, standing all clear to view in the bright moonlight of a Sicilian sky. Soon after he was able to distinguish the hut built amongst its five trunks, which all receive their sap from the same source, as a receptacle in which the abundant harvest of its fruit is in due season housed. As soon as he had nearly reached it, he thought he saw the shadow of a human being leaning against one of those trunks—another minute ended all doubt upon the subject, and he distinctly beheld the figure of a tall athletic man standing before him.

"Who's there?" said Pascal, bringing his carbine to the "present."

"A man!" replied the unexpected visiter. "Did you expect your money would come here of itself?"

"No," said Bruno; "but I did not expect that he who brought it hither, would have had the courage to wait for me to come and receive it."

"Then," said the stranger, "you know less of the Prince Butera than I thought."

"What, Sir," said Pascal, returning the carbine to his shoulder, and respectfully uncovering his head, "can it be possible that your Highness has condescended to come hither yourself?"

"Yes," said the Prince, for it was he,

"I have. A bandit may sometimes want money as well as his betters, and in that case, I should not like to refuse him; only I took it into my head to bring it, in order that the bandit might not flatter himself that I buried it here out of fear of him."

"Your Excellency," said Pascal, "is worthy the reputation you have obtained."

"And," said the Prince, "are you worthy of yours?"

"My answer to that," said Pascal, "must depend upon what you have heard of me. Men like *me,* have more reputations than one."

"Well said," cried the Prince; "your wit seems equal to your courage. I love brave men, let me meet them where I may. Listen to me—will you exchange your roving life, and the Calabrian habit, for service, and the rank of captain? Will you go fight the French? Say yes, and I will undertake to raise a company for you upon my own estates, and answer for your commission."

"Prince, I thank you," said Pascal, "your offer is noble, but I have sworn an oath to be revenged for wrongs which I have suffered, for injuries which I have received—the redemption of that oath, will keep me some time in Sicily—that once achieved, I may listen to your liberal proposal."

"Do as you like," said the Prince, "decide for yourself; but rely upon it, you had better accept my offer at once."

"Prince," said Pascal, all the recollections of the past, flashing in an instant across his mind, "I *cannot.*"

. "Well," said the Prince, " then here is the purse you asked for—take it—go to the devil with it if you will—it is at your service, only take care that you do not get yourself hanged before *my* door —all the gentlemen of your profession, who are caught, swing, as you know, on the Marina, in front of my house. It is no pleasant sight at any time, and I assure you that the agreeableness of the exhibition would by no means be increased by *your* appearance there."

Bruno took the purse, and weighing it in his hand, said, " Prince, this purse is very heavy."

" To be sure it is," said his Excellency, " do you think I would permit a fellow like you to dictate to the Prince Butera, what ought to be the extent of his liberality? You asked for two hundred ounces —— I have brought three hundred !"

" Whatever you have brought, sir," said Pascal, "shall be faithfully returned to you."

" Psha !" said the Prince, "I am not an usurer, I never lend—I always give."

" And," answered Bruno, proudly, "I borrow, or I steal, but I never lie—take back your purse, Prince. I shall apply for the loan elsewhere."

" Well," said the Prince, "you are certainly the most punctilious bandit I ever happened to meet with—however settle the affair with your own conscience, and call it a loan, if you please, for I must get home."

" Good night, Prince," said Pascal, " St. Rosalia guard you."

The Prince walked off with his hands

tucked into his before-named leathern waistcoat, whistling one of his favourite airs. Bruno remained motionless, watching him intently. When he lost sight of him, Pascal, whose heart had been moved by the Prince's offer, heaved a deep sigh, and descended the mountain on the opposite side.*

The next day, the innkeeper whose house had been burned, received the whole three hundred ounces by the hands of Ali.

* For fuller details of this extraordinary Prince Butera, see the witty and amusing recollections of *Palmieri de Miccichi.*

CHAPTER V.

It was not long after the occurrence of this extraordinary scene that Pascal obtained information that gold to a large amount was about to be transmitted from Messina to Palermo. To know *from* whom, *to* whom, and above all *why*, this money was thus to be transported, would considerably edify the uninitiated, by exposing to view the simple and summary mode in which the Sicilian taxes are levied.

The reader has been already apprized of the capture of Prince Moncada Paterna by pirates, near the village of Fugallo, on his return from Pantelleria. Immediately after he was made prisoner he and his suite were carried by the captors in the first instance to Algiers, where the terms of his ransom were arranged, according to which, the amount was fixed at five hundred thousand piasters (equal to about one hundred thousand pounds sterling), half to be paid before the Prince left Algiers, and the other half within twelve months after his arrival in Sicily.

The Prince having no alternative, wrote to his bankers, communicating the difficulty in which he was placed, and desiring them to remit the first instalment of the price of his liberty with the least possible delay. As Moncada Paterna was one of the most affluent of the Sicilian nobility, the money was forthwith raised and forwarded to Africa. The Dey, true to his promise as a faithful disciple of the Prophet, released the Prince and his suite upon the receipt of the first moiety, trusting to his honour for the payment of the second, within the stipulated period.

When the Prince found himself once more in his own territories, his first care was to make preparations for collecting from every available source the sum still wanting to enable him to fulfil the conditions into which he had entered with the Dey. But Ferdinand IV., apprized of these meritorious exertions hit upon a scheme highly creditable to his genius and talents for financial affairs. As he was at war with the Regency it was beyond measure galling to him to hear of the transfer of so large a sum of Sicilian gold to his enemies, and it struck him that as Moncada Paterna was rich enough to make a particular point of fulfilling his engagements with pirates, the treasury of Messina was a much better receptacle for the money than the coffers of those infidel plunderers; accordingly the Prince one fine day received a royal mandate to pay over the two hundred and fifty thousand piasters which he had raised, to the Government.

The Prince being a loyal and obedient subject, did not hesitate for a moment to obey his Majesty's command; but being also a man of the most rigid honour, he resolved not to prevent its fulfilment to interfere with his pledge to the Dey, to whom he actually sent the promised amount. So that in point of fact his Highness's emancipation cost him no less than seven hundred and fifty thousand piasters, two-thirds of which reached their original destination, and the remaining third was paid at Messina to the account of Prince Carini, the Viceroy. This money Bruno had heard was actually on its way to Palermo, the seat of government, escorted by a brigadier and four gendarmes. The brigadier, besides the treasure, was charged with a letter from Prince Carini to his beautiful Countess, Gemma, entreating her to come to him at Messina, where he found he should be detained by official business for some months.

On the evening when Pascal expected the money to be in the neighbourhood of Bauso, he let loose his four Corsican dogs, and taking them with him, crossed the village of which he had become the lord (at least inasmuch as his occupation of its half-ruined fortress gave him the right), and concealed himself amongst some thick underwood by the side of the road leading from Divieto to Spadafora. He had not been in his ambuscade more than an hour before the trampling of horses, and the rumbling of a waggon's wheels struck upon his attentive ear. He looked to the priming of his carbine, satisfied himself that his dagger would come easily from its sheath, and then whistling his dogs, which came and crouched at his feet, he placed himself in the middle of the road.

In a few moments the expected party turning a corner, caught sight of him; he remained firm on his ground, the leading gendarme challenged him:

" Who comes there?"

" Pascal Bruno," said the brigand.

The words were like those of magic, the four gendarmes, without waiting to make any further inquiries, instantly abandoned the treasure and their duty, and fled in dismay. Pascal's dogs, which at a signal from their master, had started to their feet, flew after them, and the brigadier was left alone and unsupported. He drew his sabre, and galloped up to Pascal. The brigand raised his carbine as steadily and coolly as if he was going to fire at a target. He waited until his enemy was within ten paces of him, his aim was taken, his finger was on the trigger, when in an instant the horse and his rider lay prostrate in the dust.

The effect upon Pascal of this sudden surprise was, however different in its character, little less powerful than that which the sound of his own name had just before produced upon the soldiers—the cause of this occurrence was, however unexpected, purely natural. The faithful Ali had, unperceived by Pascal, followed him from the fortress, and seeing the brigadier ride up to him, threw himself upon the ground, and crawling behind him, with one cut of his ataghan, succeeded in hamstringing his horse. The brigadier, entirely unprepared for the shock, lost his seat, and was pitched forward on the earth, where he now lay stunned and bleeding.

Pascal, seeing that the fall had put his antagonist completely *hors de combat,* and that nothing was to be apprehended from *him*, assisted by Ali lifted him into the waggon, and giving the reins to the young Arab, directed him to drive the vehicle up to the fortress, while he proceeded to detach the carbine from the saddle of the wounded horse, and to secure all the papers and letters which might be contained in the saddle-bags. He then whistled back his dogs, which came ramping and panting to their master's call, their eyes flashing fire, and their mouths reeking with blood ; and after this fashion the party returned to the fortress.

As soon as Pascal had got within the gates he locked them, and made all secure ; then lifting the still unconscious brigadier in his arms, he carried him to a room where there was a mattress, on which its master was in the habit sometimes of resting himself in his clothes. Upon this, Pascal deposited his living burden, and then quitted the room, having, either through forgetfulness or carelessness, left the brigadier's carbine in one of its corners.

In the course of a short time the brigadier began in some degree to recover his senses ; he opened his eyes and looked about, and, finding himself in a place wholly unknown to him, began to think that he was dreaming, and accordingly shook himself in order to ascertain whether he was really awake. Feeling a pain across his forehead he raised his hand to his eyes, and, drawing it back again, found it covered with blood. The sight of the wound brought all the circumstances of the recent affair to his mind. He now recollected that he had been stopped by one single bandit, and that, basely deserted by his dastardly followers, he had himself fallen from his horse just at the moment he was on the point of attacking his enemy—beyond that, of course, he remembered nothing.

The brigadier was a brave man and a good soldier, and, conscious of the responsibility in which he was involved, felt deeply and bitterly the conduct of those who had abandoned him. He again looked round the room in hopes of ascertaining where he was—but—no—every thing about him was new to his eyes, and utterly unknown to him. He got up as well as he was able, went to the window, and saw that it opened to the country. A thought flashed into his mind that it might be possible for him to leap from it, seek for assistance, and return with a sufficient force to

take his revenge, and even regain his lost
treasure.   With this hope strong in his
mind he had half opened the casement,
when, taking a last look of his prison,
as he justly enough considered it to be,
he beheld, to his amazement and delight,
his own carbine placed close to the bed.
The moment his eye glanced upon the
weapon his heart palpitated.   Thoughts
far different from those of flight—thoughts
of a much deeper character, fraught with
consequences of tenfold importance filled
his mind.   The chance of retribution,
prompt,   sure,   and   mortal,   offered
itself.   Satisfied that he was alone, he
eagerly caught up the weapon that had
so often done him good service in the hour
of peril.   He hastily opened the pan—saw
the priming still there—tried the barrel
with the ramrod — it remained loaded

——he was safe, and sure of his revenge. He returned the carbine to its position against the wall, and throwing himself on the bed, stretched himself out in the position in which he had found himself when he came to his senses, in order that it might appear as if he had not risen at all.

Scarcely had he resumed his place when Pascal Bruno entered the room. He had a lighted firebrand in his hand, which he threw upon the hearth, and kindled the wood which had been previously laid there. He then proceeded to a small cupboard in the wall, whence he took two plates, two glasses, two bottles of wine, and a cold roasted shoulder of mutton. He placed them on the table, and seemed waiting only

K

the brigadier's recovery to do the honours of the unexpected repast.

The room in which these events were occurring was rather longer than it was broad. At one end of it was a window, at the other end, the door; between them the fireplace. The mattress on which the brigadier lay was in a line with the window. Bruno stood before the fireplace, his eyes fixed vaguely on the door, and himself plunged in a profound revery.

This was the moment—the crisis was at hand—now was the brigadier resolved upon the cast by which all was to be won or lost—the stake was important—life against life. He raised himself upon one hand, keeping his eyes fixed upon Pascal, and cautiously stretching out his other arm, he took hold of the carbine just below the lock, and held it for a moment, alarmed by the beating of his own heart, and terrified lest the next move he made might alarm his enemy; but seeing Pascal so perfectly abstracted he took courage, and casting one look at the window as his sole means of escape after he had struck the deciding blow, supported himself on his knee, and raising the carbine, took aim at Pascal with all the steadiness and precision of one conscious that his own existence depended upon the success of a perilous enterprise—he fired.

The smoke is dissipated—the brigadier pauses where he is, for a moment, to ascertain the effect of his shot. What does he see? Bruno stooping and picking up

K 2

something from the floor, which he holds to the light to examine, and then advances towards the bed, the brigadier remaining silent and astounded at the spectacle before him.

"My good friend," said Pascal, as he approached his unwilling guest, "when next you fire at *me*, load your carbine with a silver bullet—leaden ones have a scurvy trick of flattening themselves against my body—like this one—see! However, I am glad to find you so much recovered. I am getting very hungry, but I could not think of being so uncivil in my own house as to go to supper without my visiter."

The brigadier stirred not—his hair was on end with fright, and a cold perspiration bedewed his forehead. Nor did the sudden appearance of Ali, who rushed into the room, ataghan in hand, at all tend to calm the agitation of his mind.

"What," said Pascal, " did the noise disturb you, my boy?—It was nothing. The brigadier fired his carbine, that was all; get thee to sleep, boy—sleep in peace—never fear for me."

Ali retired without saying a word, and repaired to his accustomed bed—a panther's skin stretched on the floor across the inside of the outer door.

"Well," continued Pascal to the brigadier, filling the two glasses with wine, "you heard what I said."

"I have," said the brigadier; "and since I am unable to kill you, I will drink with you though you be the devil himself." Saying which, he walked boldly up to the table, took his glass, drank to Bruno, and swallowed its contents at one gulp.

" What do you call yourself?" said Pascal.

" I am called Paolo Tommasi, brigadier of gendarmerie, at your service," said the stranger.

" Then," said Pascal, patting him on the shoulder, " you are a brave fellow ; and I will make you a promise."

" What is it ?" said the brigadier.

" Why this," replied Bruno : " that no man but yourself shall gain the three thousand ducats reward which are offered for my head."

" Gad !" said Paolo ; " but that's a capital notion."

" Yes," said Pascal ; " but the time is not come yet—I am not yet tired of life ;

on the contrary I am deucedly hungry, so let us have our supper, and we will discuss this matter further at some more seasonable opportunity."

" May one," said Tommasi—" may one make the sign of the cross here, by way of grace ?"

" With all *my* heart," said Pascal.

"I only asked," said the brigadier; " I did not know—I thought, perhaps, it might make you uncomfortable; one has doubts, sometimes."

" Do as you please," said Pascal; " make yourself at home."

The brigadier accordingly crossed himself, and began an attack upon the cold mutton with the air and appetite of a man perfectly at his ease, and who knows that under the most difficult circumstances he has done all that could be expected or required of a brave soldier. Pascal was equally agreeable and familiar; and certainly no one who could have seen these companions enjoying a *tête-à-tête* supper, helping each other to wine with every mark of good fellowship, could have imagined it possible that within the two preceding hours either of them had done his best to blow the other's brains out.

"Comrade," said Tommasi, after a brief pause in the conversation, arising from the difficulty of getting words out of his mouth, and taking cold mutton into it simultaneously, "you live well here—your wine is excellent, your welcome warm; but do you know I should enjoy them all much more if I knew when it was probable I should leave your residence, pleasant as it is."

" Probably to-morrow morning," said Pascal.

"Then," said the brigadier, " you don't intend to keep me prisoner?"

" Prisoner!" said Pascal, " what the deuce have I to do with prisoners?"

" Hem!" said Tommasi; " so far so good—but—forgive me—that, you know, is not all."

" What more?" said Pascal, again filling the glasses.

" Why," said the brigadier, looking through his glass at the lamp which Pascal had lighted, " there is—I admit it is somewhat of a delicate question—but —what—"

" Well," said Pascal, " go on."

" You won't fly into a passion?" said the brigadier.

" You ought by this time to know me

better than to think I should," said
Bruno.

" Well, then," said Paolo, " you must
recollect that when I met you I was not
alone."

" No," said Pascal ; " there were four
gendarmes with you."

"Yes," said the brigadier, "there
were four gendarmes ; but I don't speak
of them : there was, if you remember, a
certain w—wag—waggon—there, now
the word's out—a waggon."

" It is quite safe," said Pascal, " in my
court-yard."

"I have no doubt of its safety," said
the brigadier ; " but what I meant just to
observe was, that I couldn't with any degree of comfort to myself, go without it."

" But I suppose," said Bruno, " you
can conveniently go with it ?"

" With it!" said the brigadier. " What just as it is—untouched?"

" Why," said Pascal, " a small portion of it may be wanted; but I will take no more than I actually require."

" And are you much embarrassed just now?" said the brigadier, anxiously.

" I want two thousand ounces," said Pascal.

" Come," said the brigadier, brightening up at the announcement, " that I consider mighty reasonable; I doubt whether many gentlemen of your profession would be so moderate."

" Nay," said Bruno; " more than that I will take care *you* shall not suffer by the loss. I will give you a formal receipt for what I take."

" Better and better," said the brigadier. " By the way, talking of receipts,

I had some papers of importance in my saddle-bags."

"They are safe," said Bruno; "here they are: you shall have them back because I know they are important to you. The first is your commission, to which I have taken the liberty of adding a postscript, containing my opinion that so brave and well-conducted an officer deserves promotion. The next is a particular description of *my* person, in which I have ventured to make a few alterations; for example, to the list of my peculiarities I have added, 'Charmed— bullet-proof;' for the truth of which, perhaps, you may yourself be inclined to vouch. The third paper is a letter from his Excellency the Viceroy, to the fair Countess of Castel-Nuovo; and I am too grateful to that lady for the forced loan of this old castle, which nominally belongs to her, to obstruct or impede the safe delivery of her ladyship's love-letters. So there, my brave fellow, there are all your documents; and now, one parting glass to our mutual healths and then to bed. I will leave you; sleep quietly, and to-morrow by four o'clock you shall start again on your journey. Take my word for it, it is much safer in these parts to travel with money by day than by night; there are some sad fellows about; and you may not always fall into such good hands."

" You are right," said Paolo, collecting his papers, "and to my mind you have a deuced deal more of a man of honour about you than half the honourable men in the kingdom."

" I'm glad you think so," said Pascal, " you'll sleep the better for your good

opinion of me.   One thing I had better
just mention to you ; don't attempt going
into the court-yard to look after your
waggon, the airing would not be good
for your health—my dogs are loose, and
would most assuredly tear you to pieces,
and eat you by way of supper."

" Thanks for your warning," said Tommasi.

" Good night," said Pascal, retiring
and leaving the soldier the alternative of
sitting till morning, drinking the rest of
the wine, or of sleeping in perfect security, on the mattress.

The next morning, as the clock of
Bauso struck five, Pascal Bruno re-
entered the apartment, and found the
brigadier, who did not appear to have
slept much, up and ready for the start.
He led him down stairs into the court-

yard ; there stood the waggon with its horses harnessed, and beside it a capital saddle - horse, caparisoned in all the trappings of the unfortunate animal, which had the night before fallen a victim to the active interference of Ali. Pascal entreated his departing guest to accept it as a present in remembrance of their interesting meeting, and agreeable intercourse ; the brigadier did not put Pascal to the trouble of repeating his request, but, mounting the animal with considerable activity and satisfaction, cracked his whip over the heads of the team, and took his departure, apparently delighted with the amiability and liberality of his new acquaintance ; but before he was out of ear-shot, his host called out loudly to him, to desire him above all things not to forget to deliver the Prince Carini's letter to the Countess. Tommasi gaily nodded assent, and was soon out of sight.

This brigadier, who was afterwards promoted to a captaincy at Messina, to this day relates the whole of this adventure to any body who will ask him for the recital, and contends with every show of reason, and every mark of belief, that Pascal was, as he described himself, a charmed being, and as truly a sorcerer as a bandit; for that of his own personal knowledge, he knows that he had been by some superhuman agency, rendered invulnerable. Nor is it safe for any of the captain's hearers to impugn his veracity upon this important point.

Nevertheless, if our readers really wish to know how it came to pass that Pascal Bruno was not killed by Paolo Tommasi, when he fired his carbine at him, within a few paces of his body, we should say, that in all probability, when he returned to the fortress, Pascal had taken the precaution to draw the ball of the carbine, although he left the powder in the barrel. However, Paolo Tommasi still continues in the faith that it was the effect of magic.

We offer these two opinions for the consideration of the reader, whom we leave perfectly at liberty to adopt which of them he pleases.

L

CHAPTER VI.

It may easily be imagined that the reputation of Pascal Bruno was not long confined to the neighbourhood of Bauso. It spread rapidly throughout all Sicily; and the feats of the bold brigand who had made himself master of Castel-Nuovo—whence like an eagle from his eyry, he dashed into the valley either to attack the rich, or defend the poor—formed the subject of general conversation.

Just at the period of which we now speak, the Prince Butera gave a splendid fête at his palace on the Marina. Pascal Bruno, the universal subject of conversation, was naturally spoken of, nor did the prince hear the stories which his guests were relating of him without thinking of their extraordinary meeting under the gigantic chestnut.

The reader has already heard enough of the style of Prince Butera's living, and the unbounded liberality of his establishment, to comprehend what a fête given by him would be, when he had resolved to make it transcend in splendour any thing of the sort which had preceded it.

It would be ridiculous to attempt to give the details, truth to be told, they far

exceeded the most sanguine expecta-
tions of his guests, and presented to
their astonished sight, something like
a bright vision, or rather, as if Palermo (where to this hour it is remembered and talked of) had been for the
occasion converted into fairy-land.

To give life and animation to the un-
paralleled splendour of the scene—the
brilliant rooms—the beautiful bosquets—
the brightly illuminated fountains playing
in marble basins, round which the gayest
groups were dancing to the sweetest
music, the performers of which were left
invisible, all the *élite* of Palermo, and their
beautiful wives and daughters, dressed in
the most brilliant or most extravagant costumes, were invited ; some came masked,
others unmasked, but all abandoning them-

selves to the beautiful illusion of the moment, gazing on the dance with delight, or listening enraptured to the love-feeding strains by which it was accompanied.

Amongst the groups who were promenading through the saloons and gardens one especially attracted general attention. This was the party of which the beautiful Countess Gemma was the leading star, and which seemed to the eyes of the rest of the company to be composed of her willing satellites. She brought with her, fair friends who, like herself, were dressed in the costume of the nobility of the thirteenth century, so admirably adapted for the display of their fine persons. They entered the circle, the Countess leading the way amidst a murmur of admiration, ushered in by the Prince Butera himself, who, dressed as a mandarin, had received her at the door of the saloon, and was now proceeding to present her to the daughter of the Emperor of China.

Every body who heard this announcement was convinced that the result would be some new display of the Prince's exquisite taste, and the consequence was, that the new arrivals were followed by a crowd of the company, who were led by the illustrious host to the entrance of a pagoda, guarded by two Chinese soldiers, who, at a signal given by the illustrious Amphitryon, threw open the doors, and displayed to the delighted eyes of the assembly an apartment entirely fitted up in the taste of the sublime and wonderful empire, in the midst of which, upon a sort of dais, was seated the Princess of Batera, arrayed in a Chinese dress, to correspond with all the surrounding objects, and which alone had cost the Prince thirty thousand francs.

As soon as the Princess saw the Countess she came forward to receive her, followed by her imaginary court of mandarins, officers, and buffoons, forming a motley group of splendid and grotesque costumes beyond belief striking.

Prince Butera's visiters, although accustomed to gaieties, and not easily startled by display, were perfectly astonished at what they saw—they could scarcely believe their eyes, and seemed disposed to ascertain the reality of the scene by surrounding the Princess; touching her robe, which was covered with diamonds, and even ringing the little golden bells with which her Highness's pointed cap was decorated. All the admiration and attention which the beautiful Gemma had a few minutes before attracted by her charms, and the costume so well calculated to display them to perfection, were in a minute transferred to the Princess, where they appeared entirely to concentrate. The surrounding visiters were not satisfied with silent approbation, they loaded her Highness with compliments—well founded, no doubt; but amongst those who were most assiduous in expressing their raptures at her Highness's beautiful appearance, none were so loud in their praises and none so forward in sounding them, as our well-remembered friend, Captain Altavilla, who still continued a constant guest at the Prince's dinner-table, to the utter discomfiture of the Maître d'hôtel, and who, by way of masquerade, appeared upon this occasion in his full uniform.

"Well," said the Prince Butera to the Countess de Castel-Nuovo, "what do you think of the daughter of the Emperor of China?"

And here one might just pause to ask, considering the terms upon which it was notorious the Countess Gemma was living with Prince Carini, how Prince Butera received and presented her to this Chinese beauty; but it seems in liberal Sicily these matters are not so much considered. Prince Carini was viceroy, and the fête was a sort of *bal masqué*, at which, upon the principal of the proverb that, "None are so blind as those who won't see," it is probable the Countess and her friends had the *entrée*.

"I think," said the Countess, "it is extremely lucky for us, that Prince Carini is just now at Messina, for if he were here with his susceptible heart, I think it extremely probable that he would give up Sicily to the Emperor of China for the sake of his beautiful daughter, and then we should be obliged to get up a new affair of vespers to get rid of the Chinese.

At this moment Prince Moncada, dressed as a Calabrian brigand, approached the Princess, and requested, as a connoisseur, to be permitted to examine her Highness's dress.

"Sublime daughter of the sun," said the facetious Captain Altavilla, pointing to the dress of Prince Moncada, "let him look—but don't let him touch ; take care of your gold bells, and all your valuables, rely upon it this is Pascal Bruno."

The lively captain thought he had said one of his remarkably good things, but he was a good deal startled when a mask who stood near him said to him,

" The Princess might be safer in the hands of Pascal Bruno than in those of a certain Santafeda of my acquaintance. Pascal Bruno is a murderer, he is not a swindler—he is a brigand, but not a pilferer."

" That is well said, mask," exclaimed Prince Butera.

Captain Altavilla bit his lips.

" You know," said the Prince de la Catolica, "the last exploit of Pascal Bruno?"

" Not I," said Prince Moncada.

" He has intercepted the treasure

which Prince Carini had sent to Palermo," said the Prince.

" My ransom !" said Moncada.

" Yes," said the Prince, "your Excellency is doomed to the Dey."

" Not," said Prince Moncada, "unless the King requires me to pay again; I have satisfied the Dey."

" Never fear, Prince," said the mask, who had previously spoke, " you are safe; Pascal Bruno has only taken two thousand ounces; he did not want any more."

" And how, sir," said the Prince, " do you happen to know that fact?" looking at the person who had addressed him, and who appeared in the costume of Vina, an Albanian colony which, upon the capture of Constantinople by Mahomet the Second, emigrated, but has most scrupulously maintained its national habit.

"I heard it mentioned," replied the Greek, carelessly playing with his ataghan; " but if your Excellency wishes for the most authentic information, here is a gentleman who can give it you, chapter and verse."

Saying which, he pointed with his dagger to our worthy friend the brigadier, Paolo Tommasi, who, as the faithful slave of the Prince, had, after depositing the treasure, hastened to the villa of the Countess with his Highness's letter, and, not finding her at home, and being informed of her visit to the fête at Prince Butera's, availed himself of his official privilege as messenger to the Viceroy, to obtain admittance to the party, where he found himself most unexpectedly the centre of a brilliant circle, the object of general interest, and a victim to universal curiosity respecting the robbery and restoration of the money. To other men this might have been seriously embarrassing; but as we have already seen, Paolo Tommasi was not a man easily daunted or put out of his way, and the first thing he did was to give the Countess her letter.

She read it; and then, turning to Prince Butera, said, "You did not think that you were giving me a farewell fête, Prince; but so it is. The Viceroy wishes me to join him as speedily as possible at Messina. You know, sir, what a faithful subject I am. I shall start to-morrow morning." Having said which she gave her purse to Tommasi, and told him he might retire.

This, however, was sooner said than done; the poor brigadier was as closely besieged as a London lion. Every body was anxious to hear the history of his rencontre with Pascal Bruno, and the price of his emancipation from these inquirers—less, perhaps, than that which Prince Moncada paid for *his*—was a recital of the adventure, with which the brigadier was compelled to indulge his captors three or four times over, never forgetting to dwell upon the fact that Pascal was, as he himself said, bullet-proof. However, Paolo did Bruno justice upon all other points, for he not only described the manner in which he had been treated by him, but spoke in raptures of the excellent horse he had given him in return for the one he had lost. Every body who heard him tell the story was perfectly satisfied of its truth, and every body listened to it with much attention, except the gallant Captain Altavilla, who every now and then expressed his doubts as to the facts. Luckily, the Prince Butera himself came to Paolo's aid, exclaiming, " I'll answer for every ord of it ; the statements are perfectly consistent with the character of Pascal Bruno."

" Do you know him, then ?" said Prince Moncada.

" Know him !" said the old Prince, " to be sure I do. I had a long conversation with him upon your estates one night, not long since."

This most staggering announcement rendered it necessary for the Prince Butera, in order to satisfy Prince Moncada, to tell *his* story, and, accordingly, he gave the whole history of his meeting with Pascal under the Chestnut of the Hundred Horses.

When the Prince came to that part of

the story where he *lent* him the three hundred ounces, Captain Altavilla could no longer help laughing outright. "And, sir," said the captain, "does your Highness expect that he will ever repay you?"

"I do not expect it," said the Prince, "I am *sure* he will."

"Pray," said the Princess de Butera, "do tell me, for I confess I am delighted with the history of brigands and robbers, and all those kind of people, because they frighten me to death. Has any body, besides the Prince, ever seen this terrific creature?"

The surrounding guests shook their heads negatively; but the Albanian mask said, "Yes! one other has seen him—the Countess Gemma de Castel-Nuovo."

M

Gemma stood aghast; all eyes were turned upon her.

"Is that so?" said the Prince Butera.

"It is true," said the Countess, trembling like a leaf; "but I had quite forgotten it."

"I dare say Pascal Bruno has not," said the Albanian.

The Countess's admission excited such a sensation among the surrounding guests, that all attempts on *her* part to avoid giving the particulars of her interview and conversation with that extraordinary hero were equally unavailing with those of the preceding historians, and she was compelled to relate all the details of his intrusion into her room, of the Prince's having fired at him, of *course*, as *usual*, unsuccessfully; and of his revengeful murder of her maid's husband on the day of her marriage.

This story, the most terrible they had yet heard of him, left a deep impression on the minds of the auditors, who shuddered at its recital; and had it not been for the garish finery of their dresses, they would have looked more like mourners at a funeral than mirthful feasters at a fancy ball.

"Well," said Captain Altavilla, who first evinced sufficient courage to speak, "whatever other sins this fellow may have committed, his greatest crime appears to me to be his being the cause of damping the spirits of our else happy party. All his other misdoings I *might* have pardoned; but for this I vow vengeance against him."

"Are you in earnest?" said the Albanian, who still wore his mask.

"Serious as ever I was in my life,"

M 2

said the captain; "and I don't know any thing in the world I should like better than to find myself face to face with him."

"That may happen one of these days," said the Albanian.

"So much the better," said the captain. "I would gladly pay any body who would ensure me the meeting."

"You may keep your money, sir," said the Albanian; "I know a man who will procure you the introduction without fee or reward."

"Where is this worthy individual to be found?" said Altavilla, affecting a smile of incredulity.

"Come with me," said the Albanian, stepping out of the circle, and beckoning the captain to follow, "and I will tell you."

Altavilla hesitated for a moment, but feeling that he had expressed his anxiety upon the subject in terms somewhat too strong to be retracted, and apprehending that any show of disinclination on his part would compromise his reputation, he put a good face upon the business, the more especially as, in point of fact, he believed the offer to be nothing more than part of an extremely well-acted masquerade joke.

"I'm your man," said Altavilla; "all for the love I bear the ladies;" and away he went following his leader.

"This is a curious scene," said the Countess, addressing herself to Prince Butera; "do you know who this noble-looking Greek is?"

"Not I," said the Prince.

There was nobody present who did.

"I beg your pardon, Prince," said Paolo Tommasi, touching his cap with his hand, "I—"

"Well," said the Prince, "what have *you* to say, my gallant brigadier?"

"*I* know him, Prince," said the brigadier; "and ought to know him well."

"You?" said the Prince. "Who is he?"

"PASCAL BRUNO!" replied the brigadier.

At the sound of this dreadful name the Countess uttered a piercing shriek and fainted.

This event speedily put an end to the fête. The Countess was led senseless to her carriage; the company were seen hurrying off in all directions; and the consciousness that Pascal Bruno had been amongst them all the evening, and was even yet, in all probability, close to them, did not in any degree retard the expedition with which they seemed disposed to get away from the still glittering scene.

In about an hour the whole of the company had departed, and the Prince, whose high sense of gallantry and hospitality would not permit him to retire until his last guest was gone, had proceeded to his own room to arrange some papers before he went to rest, when a slight tap at the door of his apartment attracted his attention.

It was Giacomo, the maître d'hôtel, who tapped, and having obtained permission to come in, stood before his master, his eyes sparkling with a look of triumph.

"What's the matter, Giacomo?" said the Prince.

"I always told your Excellency how it was," replied the man.

"Always told me how what was?" asked the Prince.

"That your Excellency's kindness would only encourage him," answered Giacomo.

"Encourage whom?"

"Captain Altavilla," said Giacomo, with the air of an augur whose prophetic announcements have been fully verified.

"Why, what has he been at now?" said the Prince.

"Be pleased, Excellency," said Giacomo, "to remember that I mentioned to you some time since that he used regularly to pocket his silver fork and spoon when he had done dinner."

"Well, what more?" said the Prince.

"And then, Excellency," continued Giacomo, "you will please to recollect that you said, so long as he did not pocket the forks and spoons which the other guests had been using it did not matter."

"Yes," replied Prince Butera, "I recollect that perfectly well."

"I have caught him at last, Excellency," said Giacomo; "he must have been doubly active to-night—eight covers are missing since the tables were laid."

"Are you sure?"

"Confident, Prince," said Giacomo; "I counted all the plate used for the purpose."

"Oh," said the Prince, "that alters the case entirely; wait while I write my gallant friend a short note."

Giacomo obeyed, chuckling with delight at the success of his precautions, and anticipating the instant dismissal of the captain from the list of visiters at the villa.

The Prince wrote as follows:

" Prince de Butera has the honour to inform Captain Altavilla, that in proposing never to dine at home in future, he finds himself by that circumstance, deprived of the pleasure of receiving the Captain as heretofore. The Prince therefore begs the Captain to accept the accompanying trifle as a slight compensation for the change it may occasion in his domestic arrangements."

" Here," said the Prince, handing fifty ounces to Giacomo, " take these and this note to Captain Altavilla in the morning."

The steward very much approved of

the exclusion of the captain, but by no means agreed with his illustrious master in the accompanying display of generosity. He knew, however, that the laws of the Medes and Persians were not more absolute than his Highness's decrees when once made. He, therefore, only bowed and retired.

Having cashiered the captain the Prince resumed his occupation of arranging his papers, and had busied himself in that way for about ten minutes, when a slight noise again attracted his attention: it was the footstep of some one approaching: he looked up and beheld standing at the open door a Calabrian peasant, holding his hat in one hand and a bundle in the other.

"Who goes there?" said the Prince.

"'Tis I, my Prince," was the reply.

"Who is it that answers me?" asked the Prince.

"PASCAL BRUNO," replied the voice.

"Ha, Pascal!" said the Prince.—— "What brings you here?"

"In the first place, Prince," said Pascal, advancing to the table where his Excellency was seated, and emptying the contents of his hat upon it, "here are the three hundred ounces you were good enough to lend me. They were appropriated to the purpose I mentioned. The inn which had been burnt down is rebuilt; the money has been repaid."

"I am glad of it," said the Prince, "you are indeed a man of your word."

Pascal bowed.

"In the next place, Prince," continued he, "I have brought you eight silver forks and spoons, upon which your arms and cipher are engraved, which I presume to have been stolen from your Excellency, by one Captain Altavilla, inasmuch as I found them stuffed into that gallant officer's pocket."

"By Jove!" said the Prince, "this is odd enough, to think that these covers, about which Giacomo was just talking, should be restored to me by *you*. And what else have you brought me—what is in that bundle?"

"Your Excellency shall see." Saying which, Pascal untied a handkerchief, and taking out of it by its hair, the head of the late Captain Altavilla, laid it upon the table before the Prince.

"What's here?" exclaimed the Prince, "a head!—Altavilla's head!—Why what the deuce am I to do with such a present as this?"

"Whatever your Excellency thinks fit," said Pascal; "I have fulfilled my duty, and so, Prince, good night."

Saying which, Pascal made a low bow to the Prince, and retired.

When he was gone, his Excellency remained looking with a thousand mingled feelings at the dreadful spectacle before him. He then began to swing himself backwards and forwards in his arm-chair, whistling one of his favourite tunes, and resolving in his mind to be less indiscriminate in his patronage for the future. It was true the captain deserved the punishment he had brought upon himself; but then—and then the Prince left off whistling, and fell into a deeper course of thought—until at length he rang the bell—Giacomo appeared.

"Giacomo," said the Prince, "you

need not take that money to Captain Altavilla — tear the letter — keep the fifty ounces yourself, and bury this piece of carrion."

CHAPTER VII.

AT the time when the events occurred of which we are treating, that
is to say, about the beginning of the
year 1804, Sicily was in a state border-
ing on barbarism, attributable partly,
as the liberal Sicilians say, to the residence of King Ferdinand in the island,
and partly to the circumstance of its
occupation by the English. The road
from Palermo to Messina by Taormini

and Catania was not made. At that time the only tolerable road from one capital to the other, was that which ran by the sea-side through Termini and Cefalu, which is now so much deserted in favour of its younger rival, as scarcely ever to be frequented, except by artists hunting for beautiful scenery, or amateur admirers of the picturesque, in which this part of the country is so rich.

At that time, no more than at present, were any post-horses to be obtained on this line, so that travellers were obliged to "go through," as the phrase runs, either on mules, or in two-horse litters ; or, if they chose to send forward relays of horses to be stationed at every fifteen leagues, in their own carriages. This being the case, all that the beautiful Countess had to do, when

N

she received the request, or command,
or whatever it might be called of the
Viceroy, that she should go to him at
Messina, was to decide upon which of
these modes of travelling she chose to
adopt.

There can be little doubt which of
the three, a lady so born, so bred, and
so circumstanced would select ; the
result was, that she ordered her carriage
to be got ready on the following morning and sent forward relays of horses
to be stationed at Termini, Cefalu, St.
Agatha, and Melazzo.   Another precaution was adopted by the establishment of the Countess, which was to direct
the courier to take care that the people at
the inns, where the Countess was to stop,
furnished themselves betimes with plenty
of provisions for the use of her ladyship,
a precaution never to be sufficiently re-

commended in Sicily, because in the inns of themselves, there is never any thing to be found to eat, the consequence of which is, that the travellers feed the inn-keepers instead of the innkeepers feeding the travellers. This being the case, the very first advice which a stranger receives on arriving at Messina, to the last which is given him at quitting it, is to hire a cook, provide a suitable *batterie de cuisine*, and lay in at least a reasonable stock of provisions. It is true, this trifling addition to the comforts, if not the essentials of the journey adds one man and two mules to the *cortège* over and above the traveller's original calculation, which addition, calculating the expense fairly and moderately, will increase his expenses by about three ducats a day.

The English explorers of the sublime and beautiful, and who spare little to make themselves what they call "snug and comfortable"—what that is, few other nations exactly comprehend—add to the cook, and the *batterie de cuisine*, and the provisions, a tent, the carriage of which, requires a third mule; which notwithstanding our fervent admiration of Sicily the bright and beautiful, it must be admitted, if not so positively necessary on the march, as the commissariat and its officer, is a very great luxury. A tent is a valuable acquisition, inasmuch as the inns are abominable; containing not one living creature, human or bestial, capable of contributing to man's comfort, and abounding, according to general report, with thousands of others, the sole occupation of whose lives, is the torment of mankind. In most cases, the majority of the latter has been found so overwhelming in the division, that many travellers have literally been laid up for want of sleep, while the scarcity of the former has been so great, that an English party having consumed all the provisions they had brought with them to one of these hotels, held a sort of council as to whether they should eat their cook, having nothing else left, and he consequently having become of himself perfectly useless to them.

I am not prepared to state whether it was a man deeply read in the history of Sicily in ancient times, but I am tolerably certain that it was for some one extremely conversant with the present state of the island, for whom supper was preparing at the inn between Feccara and Patti, which rejoiced in the sign of "the Cross," and had been recently built upon the site of one which was burned down some time before.

The encouragement which the landlord and landlady had received might probably account for the activity and civility they displayed towards their guest. Certain it is, that directed by a strange cook who superintended the performances, they exhibited a skill and genius in the dressing of fish, game, and poultry, which would have done honour to a higher sphere, and as it was, kept the stewpans, fryingpans, and spits in full play.

This stranger, for whom all this preparation was making, was one who, so far from contenting himself with mere comforts, seemed disposed to indulge in every luxury the world affords. He had arrived from Messina with his own carriage and horses, and had stopped at the Cross, because he said he admired its situation, and the view it commanded, and having ordered them to unpack from his vehicle every thing requisite for the luxurious accommodation of a travelling Sybarite (his plate, his linen, his wine, and even still more his bread), he desired that he might be shown to the best rooms. Having taken possession of them, he ordered his attendants to light some delicious pastilles in a silver censer, which of course he had brought with him, and then stretching himself on a rich Turkey carpet, he whiled away the tedious half-hour before his repast, by smoking in a splendid cheboque, some of the finest tobacco of

Mount Sinai, while with his other hand he carelessly patted the head of a gigantic Corsican dog which lay faithfully crouched at his feet.

While he was thus orientally employed watching the odorous smoke as it rose curling from his pipe, and hanging in clouds about the ceiling, the landlord entered the room followed by a servant in splendid livery, who stopped at the threshold.

" Well, sir," said the stranger; " what do you want, where is my dinner ?"

" Excellency," said the landlord, "the—a thousand pardons—the Countess Gemma de Castel-Nuovo has this moment arrived at the door."

" Well," said the stranger, " what then ?"

" Excellency," replied the landlord,

" her ladyship has been forced to stop at my humble inn, because one of her ladyship's horses has fallen dead lame, and she cannot go on."

" Well," again said the stranger, " and what then?"

" Her ladyship," continued the landlord, " not calculating on such a mishap, when she left St. Agatha in the morning, made sure of getting to Melazzo tonight to sleep; her ladyship's next relay of horses is there, and—I beg your Excellency's pardon, her ladyship has no provisions with her, and——"

" Present my respects to the Countess," said the stranger, " my cook and what provisions I have are entirely at her ladyship's service."

" Many thanks to your Excellency, in my mistress's name," said the liveryservant; " but as her ladyship must send

on to Melazzo for horses, which cannot
be done in a minute, my lady must pass
the night here ; and the house, saving
your presence, mine host, is not much
better provided for sleeping than for
eating, and perhaps, sir—my lady bid
me mention it, you would be so good as
to—"

" The Countess," interrupted the traveller, " can do no better than take possession of these apartments completely
ready as they are. This closet will
serve for her maid, whom of course her
ladyship would like to have near her in
a strange place. As for myself, I care
nothing about it, I am used to fatigue,
and although I love my ease, can rough it
without repining—you," added he, turning
to the landlord, " can give me any other
room that happens to be disengaged. Go
down sir, therefore, to your lady, and say,

these rooms are at her service; since my worthy host will give me the best he can." Saying which, while the obsequious lackey was bowing the gratitude of his noble mistress for the stranger's generous surrender of his comforts and accommodation, the stranger whistled his dog to follow him, and taking his pipe with him, followed the landlord, who led the way to some other less splendidly prepared *salle à manger*. As for the servant, he returned to the Countess to repeat the success of his mission.

Gemma received the intelligence which he brought, with a dignified condescension, and accepted the traveller's kind offer not as a matter of extraordinary gallantry and civility, but as a Queen would receive the legitimate homage of a subject—she was so accustomed to see every one bend to her will, obey her orders, and watch over the expression of her countenance, in order if possible to anticipate her wishes, that she did not feel any thing like gratitude for the manner in which the stranger had so readily permitted himself to be deprived from the enjoyment of all the luxuries with which he had surrounded himself, and yielded to the inconveniences of one of the commonest rooms of a little inn.

Yet such was the beauty of her face, such the symmetry of her figure, such the grace and dignity of her bearing, that her influence was universally and even unconsciously admitted ; and as she moved from her carriage to the apartment destined for her reception, leaning on the arm of her waiting-woman, all the people of the house, who were drawn up to receive her, bowed reverently as she passed. There was something at once so commanding and so easy in her manner, that her power over her inferiors was irresistible. She looked beautiful in her travelling-dress, which was extremely picturesque, while to protect her from the cold of the mountains, she had twined round her neck a boa of the purest sable, an article of dress then unknown to Sicily, but which had been brought from Constantinople by a Maltese trader expressly for Prince Carini. On her head she wore a small black velvet cap, from under which flowed in all their beautiful richness, those magnificent ringlets so often the theme of praise and admiration.

Taught, as the Countess had been, by the servant's description to expect a room not altogether unworthy of her oc-occupation, she could not help expressing her surprise at the luxuries which surrounded her, and by which the stranger had contrived so speedily and effectually to overcome the native poverty of the apartment. The table was covered with plate and the finest damask, and the atmosphere was redolent with the most delicious perfumes.

"Am I not fated for happiness?" said the Countess to her maid; "when one of my horses was lamed by the stupidity of a servant, I was half inclined to suspect that he had some bad intention in causing my delay, and murmured at being obliged to stop at such a place as this; and yet, here, see! look round! surely some good Genius has pitied my entrapment, and built a fairy palace in the midst of the wilderness for my reception."

"And have you, madam," said Gidsa, her maid, "no suspicion who this amiable Genius is?"

" Not I," replied the Countess.

" I think your ladyship *might* guess," said Gidsa, significantly.

" I declare," said Gemma, throwing herself into an armed chair, "I have not the slightest idea."

" I beg a thousand pardons," said the maid ; " but perhaps you would be angry if I were to say what I think ?"

" Not I," said the Countess, " speak out, girl."

" Why then," said Gidsa, looking archly, " I think, that his Highness the Viceroy, knowing exactly when you would arrive at this point of the road, might wish to anticipate your arrival, might, perhaps, leave Messina to meet your ladyship, and *might* hear of the accident, which, perhaps, his Highness even *might* have contrived. And so——"

" I see it all !" interrupted the Countess, "rely upon it you are right; it never struck me, but now you have put the thought into my head, I am sure you have guessed it; who but he could have fitted up this room so luxuriously, only to give it up to me. But listen, Gidsa, say not one syllable of your suspicions; if the Viceroy has really invented this stratagem to surprise me, nothing would mortify him more than knowing that I had discovered his little scheme; therefore, remember I don't believe a word of your surmises, I am convinced that it is *not* the Viceroy who is here incognito; the stranger who has behaved so gallantly is an unknown traveller; so if you please, Gidsa, no more proof, no more corroborations; leave me in the ignorance in which I was, before you enlightened me. Remember, keep silence; because, if it be he, after all, I ought to have guessed it instead of you.

But it is *not* the Prince; yet," continued the Countess, perfectly convinced, notwithstanding what she said, that it *was* Rodolph, "how kind, how affectionate he is; what pains he takes to secure my happiness and comfort, how he loves me!"

"Who but his Highness," continued Gidsa, growing bold upon the credit of her penetration, "would have caused such a repast as this, to be got ready, exactly at the time when ——"

"Hush, hush," said the Countess, "I 'take the goods the Gods provide,' and say nothing, guess nothing. See! look at this splendid service; what should I have done if fate had not thrown me in the path of this magnificent traveller? what should I have done in this little inn without plate? I can eat off nothing else; it is not affectation; habit, I suppose, has made

o

it essential to my comfort. Look, too, at this magnificent cup, the work of Benvenuto, or at least equal to it; let me drink out of it, Gidsa."

Gidsa poured some water into the cup, and added a few drops of Lipari Malmsey. The Countess drank it off at a draught, less eagerly on account of her thirst, than from a desire to press the goblet to her lips; as if, when she touched its brim, some secret sympathy might tell her whether Rodolph himself had drunk from it, and whether it really was he who had anticipated the wants and wishes of a being, to whom, accustomed from childhood, to all the pomp of circumstance, such accessories were, as she herself had just admitted, absolutely essential.

The banquet, for such it really was,

whether called dinner or supper, was put down. The Countess, with all her wonted grace and elegance, sipped and tasted of various dishes, but with the appetite and fickleness of a bee or a butterfly,

Who but sips of a sweet and then flies to the rest.

thinking less of what she was eating than of any thing else in the world. Her looks were anxiously and expectingly fixed on the door; she started whenever it was opened, tears filled her eyes, her bosom heaved rapidly, an unaccountable, yet delightful languor stole over her senses, and she sank backward in her chair.

Gidsa perceived the effect which had been produced upon her lady, and enquired if she were ill.

" No," said the Countess, " not ill— but do not you find that the fragrance of

o 2

the perfumes around us are almost in
toxicating ?"

" Shall I open the window, madam ?"
said Gidsa.

" No, no," said the Countess, " stay
where you are ; I feel as if I were dying,
but such a death as this is sweet. Un-
bind my hair, Gidsa, I cannot bear the
pressure on my temples."

Gidsa obeyed, and the beautiful and
luxuriant tresses of her lovely mistress fell
over her shoulders, nearly to the floor.

" Do you feel nothing remarkable in
the atmosphere of the room ?" said the
Countess ; " it is something supernatural
which affects me, I must have swallowed
some philter, some charm ; help me up,
Gidsa, lead me to the mirror, bid the
people remove all these dishes, and then
undress me and then—leave me."

Gidsa obeyed; the Countess's servants removed every vestige of the late splendid meal, and the maid proceeded to fulfil the second article of her instructions; the Countess still remaining before the glass gazing at her own beautiful face, as she supported her head with her hands on the chimneypiece.

Gidsa continued to undress the Countess, who seemed utterly incapable of the least exertion; she scarcely moved, and with difficulty raised one arm after the other to afford her maid the opportunity of performing her task, which, however, she eventually accomplished without waking her lovely mistress out of the delicious trance into which she had fallen. Having completed her duty, Gidsa according to the Countess's command left the room. Gemma, in a state of unconsciousness, threw herself on the bed; she leant upon

her elbow for a few moments, listening,
with her eyes still fixed upon the door,
every moment expecting to see the Viceroy—but he came not; and, in spite of
all her efforts to keep awake, her head
dropped upon the pillow, and whispering
to herself his much-loved name, she sank
into a deep sleep.

When the beautiful Gemma awoke in
the morning, she stretched forth her
hand, as if she expected to find her beloved Prince beside her; but no—she
was alone — she looked round her in
amazement and in terror—a thousand
terrible thoughts filled her mind — a
letter lying on a table near the bed,
caught her eye—she snatched it up, and
read it—thus it ran:

" Countess,
        " I might have inflicted upon you,

the vengeance of a brigand; I preferred the happiness of a Prince. Lest you should flatter yourself that you have been dreaming, I have left you a lasting proof of my reality. Look in your glass, and remember

"PASCAL BRUNO."

The Countess trembled from head to to foot—the cold dew stood on her forehead—her first impulse was to ring for Gidsa, but summoning all a woman's courage, she sprang from the bed, and obeyed the dreadful order of her deadly foe. The instant she beheld herself, she uttered a faint shriek, and hid her face in her hands. Her beautiful hair had been cut short, and her eyebrows shaved off. What her feelings were at this terrible sight, confirmatory, too, of all her worst apprehensions, who can attempt to describe; she hastily dressed herself without the assistance of Gidsa, and enveloping herself in a thick veil, ordered the carriage to be got ready instantly. Luckily the relay of horses had arrived—her orders were obeyed—she hurried down the stairs and along the passage of the inn, threw herself into the vehicle, and directed the drivers to return to Palermo.

Arrived there, she instantly wrote to Prince Carini, to let him know that her priest had ordered her, by way of expiation for her sins, to cut off her hair and eyebrows, and shut herself up in a convent for the space of a year; adding, that she had actually set off to the appointed cloister to perform this pious act of repentance.

CHAPTER VIII.

On the 1st of May, 1805, Pascal Bruno being in a remarkably good humour, thought fit to have what he called a fête, in his fortress of Castel-Nuovo, and accordingly invited to sup with him, a particular friend of his, Placido Tomaselli, a highly respectable smuggler, from the village of Gesso, who was good enough to bring with him two extremely agreeable young ladies, whom he had induced to accompany him from Messina, to join the party. Upon this occasion, Pascal delighted with the delicate attentions of his visiter, resolved to " do the thing handsomely," and accordingly, the best Sicilian and Calabrian wines in his store, were drawn from the cellar, and the best cook in Bauso retained to display his skill and ingenuity, to do honour to the occasion.

The agreeable party had scarcely begun their repast, when Ali brought in a letter directed to Placido Tomaselli, which had just been delivered to him at the gate by some person from Gesso. Placido read it, and then crumpling it up in his hand, exceedingly angry, exclaimed,

" Fine time this to choose !"

"What's the matter," said Pascal, "who is that from?"

"Captain Luigi Cama, of San Gioviani."

"What," said Bruno, smiling, "our purveyor of spirits?"

"Exactly," replied Tomaselli. "He writes me word that he is on the beach, and that he wishes, if possible, to dispose of his cargo, before the custom-house officers know of his arrival."

"Business before pleasure any day," said Pascal, "go—do as he desires—you will leave me in good company. Don't stay too long, and when you return you will find all that you leave, and more than you could take with you."

"Rely upon it, I sha'n't be long," said Tomaselli, "an hour will do the business; the shore is not more than a quarter of a mile off, and—"

" And," interrupted Bruno, " we have the whole night before us."

" Good appetite to you," said Tomaselli.

" Bon voyage," said Bruno.

" Addio !"

And so they parted — Placido went his way, and his absence was little regretted. Bruno had wit and conversation for two, and there he remained with the ladies, to whom he made himself particularly agreeable ; they laughed, and talked, and sang, till at length the conversation was beginning to take a particularly lively turn, when the door opened, and a new personage of the drama made his appearance.

This was no other than a Maltese merchant with whom Pascal had some extensive dealings.

"Welcome, my friend!" exclaimed Pascal, "and trebly welcome if you bring with you some Turkish pastilles, Latakian tobacco, or Tunisian scarves—by the way, your opium did wonders."

"I'm glad on't," said the merchant; "but at the present moment, business very different from mine generally, brings me here."

"You are come to supper," said Pascal, "sit yourself down, and make yourself merry."

"Your wine is excellent," said the trader, "your guests are charming, but I have something most important to tell you."

"To tell *me*?" said Pascal.

"To tell *you*," replied the Maltese trader, somewhat emphatically.

"Well, speak then, my friend," said Pascal.

"It is for your own ear only," answered the merchant.

"Well then," said Pascal, "fall to—let us be gay, and tell me your secret in the morning."

"It must not be delayed till to-morrow," said the merchant, "you must hear what I have to say, directly."

"Well then, speak out," said Pascal, "there are no strangers here, and when I am once settled in for pleasure I cannot be disturbed, even if it were a question of life and death."

"You have hit it," said the merchant, "it *is* a question of life and death."

"Psha!" said Pascal, filling his glass, "Providence protects the virtuous. Here's to your health—drink!" the Maltese trader swallowed his bumper. "Now my friend, begin—preach, and we will listen."

The merchant, quite aware what sort of person he had to deal with, did as he was bidden.

" Well then," said the merchant, " you are perhaps aware that the judges at Calvarusa, Spadafora, Bauso, Saponara, Divieto, and Romita, have been arrested."

" I have heard such a report," said Pascal, carelessly, tossing off his bumper of Marsala, the Madeira of Sicily.

" And you know the reason why they have been arrested?" said the merchant.

" Why," said Pascal, " I should not be very much surprised if Prince Carini in a fit of ill humour brought on by his beautiful mistress's sudden retirement from the world, had taken a fancy, that their worships were either negligent, or ignorant, or perhaps worse,

in not having long before this, secured
the head of your humble servant, for
which a reward of three thousand ducats
is offered."

"Right again, Pascal," said the merchant, "that *is* the reason."

"You see," said Bruno, "I am tolerably conversant with the news of the
day."

"True," said the merchant; "nevertheless there may be certain matters
personal to yourself which have not yet
reached you."

"There *may*," said Pascal. "Om-
niscience is not an attribute of humanity—if such be the case, enlighten me,
my friend."

"Well then," said the merchant,
"these judges have raised a subscrip-
tion amongst themselves, for the purpose

of bribing some one or two of those who are in the habit of visiting you, to betray you into the hands of justice."

"Let them contribute," said Bruno, "let them offer. I'll be sworn there is not a man within ten leagues who would consent to do their dirty work."

"Do not be too sure of that," said the merchant. "The traitor *has been* found."

"Hah?" said Pascal, knitting his brows, and grasping the hilt of his dagger, "and how may you have learned that?"

"In the simplest, but most certain manner," said the Maltese merchant. "I was yesterday sent for by the Prince de Goto, whom you know is governor of Messina, who desired me to take him

P

some patterns of Turkish stuffs ; while I
was there, a servant came into the room,
and whispered in his Excellency's ear.
'That's right,' said the Prince ; 'desire
him to come in.'   The Prince then made
a sign to me to step into the next room ;
I did so, and the Prince not of course
suspecting that I was acquainted with *you*,
took no precaution to prevent my over-
hearing his conversation with his new
visiter, the whole of which was about
yourself."

"Well," said Bruno, "what did they
say of me?"

"The man who was announced," said
the merchant, "pledged himself to open
the gates of your fortress, and to secure you without opposition, while you
were at supper this very night, himself

leading the gendarmes into the room in which we are now sitting."

"Do you know this fellow?" said Pascal.

"I do," replied the merchant.

"Name him," said Pascal.

"Placido Tomaselli!"

"Tomaselli!" repeated Pascal, grinding his teeth, "why he was here but ten minutes ago."

"And has he gone out?" said the merchant.

"He went out," said Pascal, "just as you came in."

"Then," said the merchant, "he is at this moment gone to fetch the gendarmes. The time is that which he himself named to the Prince. You had just sat down to supper as he went—this all corresponds with his avowed intentions: rely upon it you have not an instant to lose.   In a quarter of an hour, flight will be impossible."

"Flight!" said Pascal, contemptuously.   "Fly! — *I* escape! — No, no! Ali, my boy—Ali!"   Ali instantly stood before him to receive his commands. "Bolt the gates; untie three of the dogs; turn them loose in the court-yard, bring the fourth, my brave and faithful Lionna to me, and then get up plenty of ammunition."

This note of preparation rang discordantly enough in the ears of the ladies, who immediately began to cry.   "Ah!" said Bruno, with an air of authority, "be quiet, my angels.   I want no more singing to-night. Be silent, and that instantly, if you please."   The terrified women were mute in a moment.   "Here, my friend," continued Bruno, addressing the merchant, "do me the favour to keep these ladies company; as for me, I must go my rounds."

Pascal took his carbine, slung on his cartouch-box, and proceeded towards the door; but, just as he was about to go out, he stopped suddenly, and listened.

"What is it?" said the Maltese.

"Don't you hear my dogs barking?" said Pascal. "The enemy are advancing — they must have been close behind you. Ar'n't they good beasts? Silence, my tigers," added he, opening the window and whistling to them. "That's right, I knew it was so."

The dogs ceased their noise, the women and the Maltese merchant began to tremble most unequivocally, presuming, naturally enough, that something terrible was about to happen.

Ali as he was ordered brought in Pascal's favourite dog, Lionna. The noble animal ran to her master, and, jumping up, placed her fore-paws on his shoulders, and looking wistfully in his face, began to growl in an undertone.

" Yes, Lionna," said Pascal, patting her affectionately, " you are a charming brute." The faithful animal growled again. " Come, then, beauty," said Pascal, " time presses ; come, come along." Pascal quitted the room, followed by his noble dog, leaving the merchant and the ladies to make it out as well as they could.

He went down into the court-yard, and found the other three dogs anxiously prowling about, but not giving signs of any immediately approaching danger. He then opened a door which led to the garden, with a view of searching that part of his domain, in case the enemy should make his advance by that route. The moment he entered it, Lionna stopped dead short, snuffed the wind, and ran off at full speed to one corner of the enclosure. When she reached the wall she made an effort to scale it, gnashing her teeth and snarling violently. She paused, and turned to see where her master was—he was close behind her.

This movement satisfied Pascal that a stranger was concealed within a few yards of them, and recollecting that the window of the room in which Paolo Tommasi had been imprisoned immediately overlooked the spot to which Lionna's attention had been directed, he instantly returned to the castle, and running up stairs, followed by Lionna, whose foaming mouth and fire-flashing eyes gave dreadful evidence that she anticipated the intentions of her master, crossed the room in which his quaking guests were huddled together, and entered the next chamber, in which there was no light, but of which the casement was open. Lionna crawled along the floor, quietly and couchingly, till within a few feet of the window, when at one spring, and before Pascal had time to check her, she darted like a panther through it, regardless of its height from the ground. Pascal was at the window in an instant after: he saw the furious animal make three bounds towards a solitary olive-tree, and drag by the throat, from behind it, a man who had there concealed himself.

"Help! help!" cried a voice, which Pascal knew to be that of Placido Tomaselli, "call off the dog. Bruno! call off the dog, or he will tear me to pieces."

"Halloo! halloo! at him, Lionna—at him!" cried Pascal. "Down with the traitor! Drag him down, my dog."

Placido who was now convinced that Pascal had discovered his treachery, and roaring with pain and apprehension, exerted all his energies to resist his gigantic enemy, while her master, leaning on his carbine, was anxiously watching the savage conflict from the window. At length, by the uncertain light of the moon, he saw two bodies struggle, fall, and rise—rise and fall again; but they were so closely grappled with each other that he could not distinguish the form of either. For ten minutes did this fearful combat last, amidst the mingled yells and cries of man and beast. At the end of that period, after a dreadful struggle, one dying shriek was heard, one form fell to the earth, but rose not again.   It was the MAN!

Pascal whistled to his avenger, passed again through the supper-room, and ran down to the door of the fortress to let her in. She was bleeding from several wounds inflicted by Placido's knife, and even from bites, which the poor wretch, in his agony, had vainly inflicted upon his triumphant antagonist. Pascal, however, had no time to attend to her then; for, as he opened the gate to give her admittance, he saw the moon's rays beaming full upon the musket-barrels of the soldiers, who were marching up the road which leads from the village to the castle.   Having secured the gate he returned to the supper-room and his trembling guests.   The Maltese drank some wine; and the two women said their prayers.

"Well!" faltered the merchant.

"Well?" replied Bruno.

"Where is Placido Tomaselli?" asked the Maltese.

"*His* business is settled," replied Pascal; "but the thing is not over yet, another legion of fiends will be on us forthwith."

"Who are they?" said the Maltese.

"Why," said Pascal, "as near as I can guess, the gendarmes, and a company of soldiers from Messina."

"And what do you mean to do now?" said the Maltese.

"In the first place, I mean to kill as many of them as I can," said Bruno.

"And what next?" asked the Maltese.

"Set fire to the fortress, and blow

myself up with the rest of them," said Bruno.

Whereupon the ladies sent forth a most piteous yell.

" Ali," said Pascal, " conduct these ladies to the cellar, let them have every thing they ask for except a light, for fear they should set fire to the powder-barrels and blow up the place before the proper time."

The unfortunate women fell upon their knees.

" Come, come," said Bruno, stamping with his foot; " obey—go—do as *I* command;" and this he said in such a tone, and with such a look, that the poor girls got off their knees as fast as they could, and without making the slightest further complaint or remark, followed Ali to the place of their destination.

"And now, my friend," said Bruno, the ladies having retired, "the best thing you can do is to blow out the light, and stow yourself away in some snug corner, where the bullets are least likely to hit you, for the musicians have arrived, and the tarantella is about to begin."

CHAPTER IX.

In a few minutes Ali came into the room, bringing on his shoulder two or three muskets, all of the same calibre, and a basket full of cartridges; Pascal opened all the windows, so as to command the enemy on every side of the fortress. Ali posted himself at one of them with one of the muskets.

" No, my boy," said Pascal, in a tone of parental affection; " *that* must not be, this affair concerns *me* alone ; *your* fate must not be linked with mine, nor will I drag you down with me and my fortunes ; you are young, and have as yet committed no crime to drive you from the world."

" Father," said the boy, " why may I not defend you as Lionna does? I have but *you* in all the world, and if *you* die I will die with you."

" No, Ali, no," said Pascal ; " if I die soon I shall probably leave behind me some mysterious and terrible mission to be executed on earth, which I can confide to no one but to you, my boy ; my child, therefore, must live to execute his father's dying orders."

" So be it then," said Ali, " the father is the master—the son will obey him."

Pascal let fall his hand; Ali took it and kissed it.

"But can I do nothing to serve you now, father?" said the boy.

"Yes," said Pascal, "load the muskets."

Ali began his operations.

"And what can *I* do?" said the Maltese from the corner, in which he had carefully ensconced himself.

"Why," said Pascal, "as for you, my friend, I shall employ you as a negotiator with the enemy, if it comes to that."

Pascal at this moment saw the muskets of a second body of men glistening in the moonlight, as they descended from the mountains; they were marching so directly towards the olive-tree, under which Tomaselli had expiated his treachery, that no doubt remained in Pascal's mind that that tree was the appointed place of rendezvous. The leading men of this detachment, when they reached the appointed spot, stumbled over the corpse ; those who followed immediately closed upon them, and formed a circle round it, but so completely had the irresistible attack of Lionna disfigured the poor wretch that nobody could recognise the defunct Tomaselli. Yet as this was the place appointed by him for their meeting, and as no other human being, living or dead, was in sight, they naturally came to the conclusion that he was the sufferer. The soldiers who began to argue the point, felt convinced that Placido's treachery had been discovered, and that consequently Bruno would be on the alert, and ready to give them a warm reception ; this convic

Q

tion acting on their minds, combined with the generally-received idea of Pascal's superhuman power, in some degree retarded their progress.

Pascal was watching all their movements from one of the windows, and just at the moment when they seemed rather undetermined as to the course they should pursue, a single ray of light from the moon happened to glance over his figure, and one of the soldiers caught sight of him, and pointed him out to his comrades. A cry of "The bandit! the bandit!" flew through the ranks, which was instantly followed by a volley of musketry. Some of the balls struck and flattened themselves against the walls; some rang in the ears of the culprit at whom they were aimed, and lodged in the rafters of the ceiling. Pascal replied to this general salute by deliberately firing four muskets from the window at the party before him, four of whom measured their lengths upon the ground.

The soldiers, who were not troops of the line, but a kind of national guard, organized for the protection of the roads, were rather " taken aback " by the fate of their comrades. These men had been fully impressed with the belief, that having secured the assistance of Placido, they were to be led into the fastnesses of the castle, and make their capture without the least resistance. Instead of which, they found that they had actually to undertake a siege, wholly unprovided as they were with any of the *matériel* for such an enterprise. The walls of the little fortress were high, the gates substantial, and they had neither ladders to scale the one, nor axes to force the other; they therefore placed their whole reliance of success upon the chance of killing Pascal when he presented himself at the window: a poor consolation for men who were firmly convinced of his invulnerability. The first movement they made was to place themselves out of reach of his musket-shot, in order to deliberate the more coolly upon the best mode of proceeding; but even this manœuvre was not performed with sufficient celerity to prevent the loss of two more of their number, who fell by the unerring bullets of Pascal Bruno.

Pascal, finding himself relieved from the immediate presence of this party, instantly removed to the windows which overlooked the village. The firing which had already occurred had alarmed the first detachment who arrived by that route, and the moment he presented himself on the other side of the castle he was saluted with a shower of balls quite equal in force and power to that with which he had been greeted in his former position. His wonderful good fortune, however, still clung to him, and he remained untouched. The effect produced by his preservation from harm upon this occasion was equal to that which had operated upon the other party — these now believed him to be magically protected, a belief which became the more implicit when they saw how regularly and with what deadly success every shot *he* fired told upon their ranks.

Although the cause of the disorder into which this second body of men was thrown, by what they considered the irresistible power of Pascal, was very similar to that which operated upon those on the other side of the castle, the effect was diametrically opposite: instead of retiring, these men placed themselves immediately under the wall of the fortress, so that it was impossible for Pascal to fire at them effectually without exposing half his body by leaning out of the window; this course of proceeding, whatever his consciousness of the magical power he was said to possess might have been, he considered a very unnecessary exposure of his person; thus, as it happened, the prudential movements of the besieger and the besieged put an end to the firing for a short time.

"Are they gone?" said the Maltese merchant, delighted at the tranquillity which was re-established. "May we claim the victory?"

"Not exactly," said Pascal; "it only

amounts to a suspension of hostilities : they have probably sent down to the village for ladders and hatchets, and I dare say we shall soon have news of their arrival; however, my good fellow, never mind, we cannot live quietly with *them*, and I don't think they will be too much at their ease with *us*." Saying which, he filled two glasses of wine, and giving one to the Maltese merchant and taking the other himself, turned to Ali and ordered him to bring up a barrel of gunpowder. Ali went to obey his instructions. "Your health, governor," said Pascal, bowing gaily to the Maltese.

"What in the name of fortune are you going to do, my dear sir, with a barrel of gunpowder?" said the Maltese merchant.

"Do? my dear friend," said Pascal; "not much—you'll see."

Ali came into the room hugging his formidable burden.

"So," said Pascal, "that's right—now, Ali, take a gimlet and bore a hole in it."

Ali proceeded to do as he was ordered with a quickness which clearly and distinctly marked his readiness to obey Pascal's directions to the letter. While this operation was in progress Pascal took one of the napkins from the table and tore it up in strips, tied them together, and having moistened them and rolled them in the powder shaken from the end of a cartridge, thrust one end of the train into the hole in the barrel and then stopped it up altogether, with some more powder, wetted. Scarcely had he completed these preparations before the sound of the hatchets chopping at the gates broke upon his ear.

" I think," said Pascal Bruno, " I am not entirely a bad prophet," rolling the barrel towards the door of the room, which opened on the staircase leading to the court-yard· He then went to the fire and took up a still burning pine-branch.

" Ah!" said the Maltese, looking as pale as death, " now I begin to comprehend what you are going to do."

" Father," said Ali, " they are coming on the mountain side with ladders."

Bruno ran to the window whence he had first fired at them, and saw, sure enough, that they had procured the means of escalade, and, shamed by their past retreat, were advancing upon the fortress with perfect steadiness.

" Are the muskets loaded, Ali?" said Pascal.

" Yes, father," said Ali, giving him his own carbine. Bruno took the weapon mechanically, and, without looking at it, lifted it slowly to his shoulder, and having taken a longer aim than usual, fired; one of the two men who were carrying the ladder fell; another took his place, a second shot from Pascal stretched him beside his comrade. Two others succeeded, and two others were killed in their turn. The scaling party then abandoned their ladder, and again retreated after firing a parting volley, which proved as inefficient as their others.

Those who attacked the gate, however, were most active and assiduous; the dogs barked fearfully, until the very sound of the blows was drowned in their noise. At length one half of the gates gave way; two or three men rushed through the opening, but their cries of distress soon convinced their comrades that they had encountered enemies of a more fearful character than they had counted upon. It was impossible to fire at the dogs without risking the lives of the men ; some of the best soldiers amongst them forced their way into the court, which, being small, was immediately filled with a crowd of troops, all engaged in a sort of Olympic combat with the noble enemies who defended the passage of the staircase leading to the room in which Bruno had established himself. All at once the door at the head of this staircase was opened and the barrel of powder prepared by Bruno came bounding down, step by step, until rolling amongst the mass it exploded, like a tremendous shell, in the midst of the motley crowd, dealing destruction all around. A considerable portion of the wall of the courtyard fell, and when the smoke cleared away not one human being within its enclosure was to be seen alive.

For a moment the besiegers on the outside were paralyzed: they however rallied: they mustered three hundred strong; and irritated by what had happened, and fired with indignation at the idea that such a body should be kept in check by a single individual, they evinced the greatest anxiety to push forward. The officers who commanded them took advantage of this good feeling, and pointed to the breach which the explosion had made practicable in the wall; they marched up to it in good order, and deploying on their front occupied its whole space; thence dashing onwards they overcame all the difficulties which opposed them, and pressing through, found themselves in the court-yard fronting the entrance.

Here the men again faltered, until some one or two of the bravest rushed up and were followed by their comrades. The staircase was theirs; a strong door which faced them was forced open; cheers of victory rang through the supper-room as they obtained possession of it; a second door was before them: it flew open at their approach, and exhibited to their view Pascal Bruno, seated upon another barrel of gunpowder similar to that which had already done such dreadful execution, with a pistol in each hand. At the same moment the Maltese merchant rushed from his hiding-place, and in a tone which proclaimed the sincerity of his apprehensions, exclaimed,

"Back! back! my fine fellows—the fortress is undermined—one step forward and we shall all be blown to atoms!"

In an instant the door was shut again, the shouts of victory were changed into yells of terror; *sauve qui peut* was the word, and the main body of troops rushed pell-mell helter-skelter down the stairs, while some, more active in their exertions towards self-preservation leaped from the windows, and in less than five minutes every living man had evacuated the fortress, of which Pascal once more found himself master. The Maltese merchant, however conducive to this result his exclamation might have been, was amongst the number who precipitately quitted the building at this most favourable opportunity.

Pascal, finding all tranquil again, rose

from his perilous seat and went to one of the windows, whence he perceived that the siege was about to be converted into a blockade ; strong parties of soldiers were posted opposite the different entrances of the castle, the men composing the different parties being sheltered from his fire by waggons and barrels. Pascal laughed at this change of system, and the new kind of warfare in which he was to be engaged.

"They are going to starve us, Ali," said he to his faithful boy.

" Dogs !" said Ali.

" No, no," said Bruno, "call them not dogs—do not insult the poor faithful beasts that died defending *me,* by comparing them with those—call them men."

" Father," said Ali.

" My boy."

" Do you see the light ?"

"It is the dawn of day," said Pascal. "Yet, it cannot be; besides the light is in the north—not the east."

"The village is on fire," said Ali.

"By St. Rosalia so it is!" exclaimed Pascal.

At this moment cries of distress were heard in the valley; Pascal rushed to the door and opened it, and found himself accosted by his friend the Maltese merchant, whose absence he had never remarked.

"Oh," said Pascal, "this is you—outside—ha! ha!"

"Don't misunderstand me," said the Maltese; "I came to you first as a friend, I come as a friend now."

"You were welcome to come," said Pascal, "welcome to go—and are welcome to return. What is happening?"

"The soldiers," said the Maltese,

" are so enraged at not having been able to take you that they have set fire to Bauso, and swear it shall burn until the inhabitants give you up."

" And the inhabitants— ?" said Bruno.

" Refuse," said the Maltese.

" I knew it," replied Bruno; "they would rather have their houses burned to ashes than touch a hair of my head. That's noble—brave—generous of them. Now go back to those who sent you here, and tell them to extinguish the fire."

"How so?" said the Maltese.

" These people and their property must be saved," said Pascal; " I will surrender myself."

" Father !" said Ali.

" Yes," said Pascal ; " those who are true and faithful to me shall not suffer by me—I will give myself up; but I have pledged my word not to deliver myself to any human being, save one. Tell them to stop this conflagration, and send to Messina for a man I shall name."

" Who is *he?*" said the Maltese.

" Paolo Tommasi, a brigadier of gendarmerie," said Pascal.

" Is there any other condition you have to make?" said the Maltese.

"One only," said Pascal; and he whispered something in the ear of the Maltese.

"Oh, father! father!" said Ali, "I hear you; do not ask them to spare my life."

" Boy," said Pascal, "have I not told you that I have need of your assistance after my death?"

"Forgive me, father," said Ali, "I had forgotten."

" Go," said Pascal to the Maltese,

"make known my terms, and if I see the fire extinguished, I shall know they are accepted. I told you, you should be my negotiator — see, it has come to pass. By the way," added Pascal, "how many houses have they burned?"

"But two, when I left the village," said the Maltese.

"Here," said Bruno, "here in this purse are three hundred and fifteen ounces —distribute them amongst the sufferers —they are brave fellows—now go, and check this calamity. Farewell!"

"Adieu!" said the Maltese merchant, shaking Pascal by the hand. He returned to Bauso.

Bruno threw his pistol away from him, and reseating himself on the barrel of powder, fell into a profound reverie.

Ali stretched himself on his tiger-skin, and lay quiet, closing his eyes, as if he were asleep, but in fact, attentively watching Bruno. By degrees the fire in the village diminished, and at last faded altogether; Pascal's conditions were accepted, and the people of Bauso rescued from the calamity with which they were threatened.

An hour had scarcely elapsed, when the door of the room opened, and Paolo Tommasi stood before him.

"Ah!" said Pascal, "Tommasi, you are here already. It is quite a pleasure to send for such a punctual man—you did not keep me waiting long."

"No," said Paolo, "they found me within a quarter of a league of Bauso, whither I was marching with my company; of course I came as fast as I could, for they told me, you wanted to see me."

"That's true," said Pascal, "I wished to prove myself a man of my word."

"I know that already," said Paolo.

"Well then," said Pascal, "I promised you once to put three thousand ducats in your pocket—you will now get them, that's all."

"Mercy on me!" exclaimed Paolo, "is it for *that,* I have been sent hither?"

"To be sure," said Pascal, "why not? What's the matter?"

"Why," said Paolo, "I would rather get three thousand ducats, by any other means."

"Why?"

"Because," said Paolo, "you are a brave man, and brave men are scarce nowadays."

"Psha!" said Pascal, "what am I to

you?—three thousand ducats will be of great use to you."

"So they will," said Paolo; "but—then—and—you mean really to surrender yourself?"

"I *do* surrender myself," said Pascal.

"To *me*?" said Tommasi.

"To you, and no one else," said Pascal. "If I had not made that promise, one of the balls which lie here, might have ended the whole of my history—but no, my word was pledged—I am your prisoner."

"You are in earnest?" said Tommasi.

"As much as ever I was in my life," said Pascal. "So now you may tell those vagabonds who are under my walls to go about their business—I want to have nothing further to do with them."

Paolo Tommasi went to the window and told the gendarmerie that they might go, for that he would be answerable with his life for the safe custody of the prisoner to Messina. A shout of exultation followed this announcement.

"Now," said Bruno, "my good brigadier, sit yourself down, and let us finish the supper, which these foolish meddlers interrupted last night."

"With all my heart," said Paolo, "for I have marched eight leagues since sunset, and am completely knocked up."

"Well," said Bruno, "if that be the case, since we have only one night to pass together, it seems right and proper that we should pass it merrily.—Ali, boy, go, fetch the ladies out of the cellar, if they are still alive—and before they come, let us drink to your speedy promotion."

Five days after this scene occurred,

Gemma the beautiful, completed the period of her religious seclusion. She had rejoined the Prince Carini, and it was in *her* presence he received intelligence of the capture of Pascal Bruno, and of his having been safely lodged in the prison of Messina.

"So much the better," said the Prince. "The Prince de Goto will pay the three thousand ducats reward — let him be tried and executed there."

"Oh!" said the lovely Gemma, in that melodious voice, and with that winning manner which were always irresistible, "I would give the world to see that Pascal Bruno, of whom I have heard so much, but whom I never could have come in contact with."

False as were these words, the appeal was irresistible.

" My beloved," said the Prince Carini, gazing with rapture upon the beautiful, sincere, and interesting Gemma, " you shall be gratified—Pascal Bruno shall be hanged at Palermo."

CHAPTER X.

ACCORDING to the promise made by the gay and gallant prince to his beautiful favourite, orders were issued to the proper authorities to remove Pascal Bruno from Messina to Palermo, whither he was accordingly conveyed under a strong military escort, and lodged in the prison of the latter city, which is situated in the rear of the Palazzo Reale, and adjoining the Lunatic Asylum.

On the evening of the second day after the arrival of Pascal in this new abode he was visited in his cell by a priest. Pascal immediately rose from his seat, and received his reverence with every proper mark of respect; but when he entered upon the purpose of his coming, and began· to impress upon Pascal's mind the absolute necessity which existed for his confessing himself previous to his execution, the brigand most earnestly protested against any such proceeding. The priest, satisfied that no attempt of his to induce him to alter this determination would be successful, contented himself by enquiring the reasons which had led him to it.

"My motive," said Pascal, "for refusing to confess, is the unwillingness I feel to commit an act of sacrilege."

"I do not comprehend you, my son," said the priest.

"Is it not an essential article of our faith,' said Pascal, "that the penitent should not only confess his own sins, but also forgive those who have sinned against him?"

"Assuredly is it," said the priest, "without it, no confession can be perfect or available."

"Well then," said Bruno, "there still live those, whose injuries done to me and mine I can never forgive; my confession, therefore, would, by your own admission, be unavailing."

"Are you not rather deterred," said the priest, "by the apprehension that you have crimes of your own to reveal which are past the hope of pardon? Comfort yourself, my son, the judgments of Heaven are tempered by mercy, and where true repentance exists hope never dies."

"Still," said Bruno, "it would be all in vain, I know my own weakness. I feel my own wrongs, and even were I to confess now, between this hour and that of my death, one ruling evil thought would have way, too powerful for me to restrain it."

"Can you not banish that thought from your mind?" said the priest.

"Banish it!" said Pascal, smiling, "no. It is upon *that* hope, *that* thought, I have lived for months and years — upon that infernal thought— the last dear hope of vengeance. Without *that,* could I have borne the existence I am now suffering? what else would have induced me to brave the ignominy of a public execution, to be made a show of, for the multitude, when I could have strangled myself in the chains with which they have bound me. I had decided upon doing so at Messina when the order for my removal hither arrived—I then felt sure SHE wished to see me die."

" Who ?" said the priest.

" SHE," said Pascal, emphatically.

" But," said the priest, earnestly, " if you die thus, without repenting—believe me, there is mercy yet"—

" Stay, father, stay," said Pascal; " SHE will also die without repenting, for death will fall upon her when she least expects it. She like me will forfeit all claim, all hope of mercy, and our fates and tortures will be the same."

At this moment one of the gaolers entered and announced that the chapel was ready lighted for the service of the dead.

"Do you persist in your determination?" said the priest.

"I do!" replied the culprit calmly, but firmly.

"Then," said the priest, "I must no longer delay the mass which I am about to perform for you. I hope that even yet, and while you listen to it, you may be inspired with better thoughts."

"It may be so," said Pascal, "but I doubt it greatly."

The gendarmes entered the cell, released Pascal from his fetters, and escorted him to the church of St. Francis de Sales, which stands immediately opposite to the prison, and which was brilliantly lighted up for the occasion. Here it was that Pascal was, according to custom, to hear the service of the dead performed, and subsequently to remain and pass the night in devotion; for the execution was to take place at eight o'clock the next morning.

An iron ring had been fixed to one of the pillars of the choir, to which Pascal was fastened by a chain, which encircled his body, but which was sufficiently long to admit of his reaching the railings of the altar, on the step of which the faithful kneel to receive the sacrament.

Just as the service was beginning, the attendants from the neighbouring lunatic asylum brought into the church a bier, on which lay the remains of one of the female patients, who had died during the day. The head of the establishment thought, it seems, that the soul of the departed might receive the benefit of the service about to be performed in behalf of that of the yet living bandit, and that such an arrangement would save the priest both time and trouble; as this appeared to suit the convenience of all parties, nobody thought fit to question its propriety. The Sacristan proceeded to place a lighted taper at the head of the corpse (which was deposited in the centre of the church), and another at the feet, and the mass began.

Pascal listened to it throughout with great attention, and when it was over the priest went to him, and inquired whether he felt conscious of any favourable change of feeling; but Pascal told him that, in spite of all he had heard and in spite of the earnestness with which he had prayed, he could not overcome the deep-rooted feelings of hatred with which the cruelty of others had inspired him. The priest promised to revisit him at seven o'clock the next

s

morning, in the hope that a night of solitude and reflection passed in the church and before the cross might by that time have worked a change in his sentiments, a consummation devoutly to be wished.

One by one the attendants quitted the church, and at length Pascal Bruno remained alone. Then it was that the whole course of his life, from his earliest childhood, past in review before him. In vain did he seek in the conduct of his boyish days for any act of his which could justly have entailed upon him the fate with which his after life was clouded; he recalled nothing in his behaviour then, but affection and obedience towards his excellent parents, in that humble happy home, which in one fatal hour had, while he was yet too young to know the cause of its change, become a scene of shame and sorrow. He recollected the day when his father left that home armed with a dagger, and when he saw him return covered with blood. The circumstances of the dreadful night in which that father was apprehended as a murderer were still fresh in his mind; and when they carried him—himself—a child, to the *Chapelle ardente,* like that in which he now stood—he saw the father he had loved, respected, and obeyed, chained as he himself was at that moment. It seemed to him that some baleful influence, some dreadful triumph of evil over good, had withered the happiness and hopes of a once virtuous family!

Upon this apparently undeserved visitation Pascal grounded those doubts which he entertained with regard to futurity. He was unable to trace the workings of Providence in the evils which had befallen his kindred; but in the anxiety of this awful moment to receive, if possible, some assurance of that felicity which is promised hereafter to those who have faith, he threw himself on the floor of the church, and, humbling his forehead in the dust, prayed earnestly and fervently that his doubts might be dispelled, his confidence here increased, and his hopes for hereafter strengthened. The days of miracles are over—all remained still and silent as the grave, except the beating of Pascal's heart, which seemed to mutter vengeance! vengeance! vengeance! He raised himself from the floor, distressed, and (such was his blindness) almost disappointed, that his earnest appeal to Heaven remained unnoticed. The mental conflict he had undergone had given him more pain than he anticipated even from the death - struggle on the scaffold. His eyes rested on the corpse which lay stretched on the bier.——In Italy the faces of the dead remain uncovered, till the moment the body is lowered into the grave. Pascal saw by the dress that it was a woman, but he was unable to distinguish the features, in consequence of a corner of the winding-sheet having fallen over the countenance of the unfortunate object before him.

A thrill of horror ran through his veins —a maddening thought flashed across his mind—he had recognised the officers of the lunatic asylum as they bore in the body. Of that asylum his beloved Teresa had been for three years an inmate. She had never recovered her senses from the dreadful hour in which her early lover became the murderer of her husband. Teresa, his betrothed! What! did he find himself now with her, dead, at the foot of the altar to which he had so fervently hoped to lead her when living? Could his evil destiny have pursued him thus far, as if in bitter derision of his misery, to unite in death those whom in life were so barbarously separated? The thought had taken full possession of him—he felt assured that the corpse before him was that of Teresa. The doubt was insupportable. He rushed towards the coffin, when, just as he was within reach of it, he felt himself suddenly pulled backwards.

The chain by which he was fastened to the pillar was not sufficiently long to permit him to touch the winding-sheet, in order to remove it from the face of the corpse. He stretched out his arms towards it—he called upon the name of Teresa. He looked round in hopes of finding something with which he could reach the coffin and unveil the features of its lifeless tenant. He endeavoured, by every exertion of his breath, to remove the fold, but it still remained in its place like marble.

Baffled in all his efforts, Pascal's rage became unbounded. He seized his chain with both hands, and, exerting his giant-like strength in all its force, endeavoured to rend his bonds asunder. But all in vain. The rings were too firmly riveted, and Pascal, discomfited and defeated, threw himself at the foot of the pillar, and, with his head resting on his hands, remained motionless and silent, a living statue of dejection and despair. Nor did he change his position until the priest returned at the appointed hour.

The reverend father approached him with a calmness and serenity truly characteristic of one coming on a mission of peace, in the hopes of reconciling man with Heaven. He thought Pascal was asleep: he placed his hand on his shoulder. Pascal started and looked up at him.

"Well, my son," said the priest, "are you ready for confession? I am prepared to absolve you."

"I will answer that question presently," said Pascal; "but first do me one service——it is the last which perhaps I shall require."

"What is it?" said the priest.

Pascal rose, and taking the priest by the hand, led him as nearly to the coffin, as the length of his chain would permit, and pointing to the corpse, said,

"Father, lift the winding-sheet from that face." The priest did as he was asked to do—Pascal was right—IT WAS TERESA. He gazed on her altered countenance for a moment with an expression of the deepest grief — he then made a sign to the priest to replace the sheet—the priest did so.

"Well," my son, said the priest, "has the sight of death awakened any pious thoughts in your mind?"

"Father," said Pascal, in a tone of thrilling anguish, " she—that woman and I, were born to be happy and innocent—*she*—she that I spoke of last night—*she* made my lost Teresa a perjurer, and me a murderer—*she* has driven us, the one by madness, and the other by despair, to

the untimely graves, which we shall fill
this day. God may pardon her—I never
can!"

At this moment, the guards entered
the church to escort Pascal Bruno to the
scaffold.

CHAPTER XI.

———

THE sky was bright and splendid, the air clear and fresh. The people of Palermo awoke as if it were a festival. It was proclaimed as a holiday at the colleges and schools, and the entire population seemed to be assembled in the street of Toledo, along the whole line of which Pascal had to proceed from the church of St. Francis, where he had passed the night, to the place of execution on the Marina.

Ladies of the first quality abandoned their beds long before their accustomed time, and nuns from all the different convents in Palermo were seen flitting like shadows in the balconies, behind the *jalousies*—for it should be understood that these immolated beauties who are not permitted to mix in the gaieties of worldly amusements, nevertheless take great delight in looking on. Every tolerably rich convent in Palermo, has, in some house or other, a floor, the windows of which, open into the street of Toledo. This floor, hired for the purpose, is connected with the convent by subterranean passages, sometimes a quarter of a mile in length, by means of which communications, the holy recluses, are enabled without sin or scandal to become spectators of all the processions sacred and profane which take place in that fascinating city.

The common people covered the flat roofs of the houses, which commanded a view of the street and place of execution, and waved to and fro like fields of standing corn. A cart drawn by mules waited for Pascal at the church-door; it was preceded by the brotherhood of the White Penitents, the first of whom bore the cross, and four others the bier.

Then came the executioner on horseback holding in his hand a scarlet flag, his two assistants, walking one on either side of him, the procession being closed by the brotherhood of Black Penitents. It passed slowly along between double ranks of regular troops and gendarmerie ; by the side, and in the middle of the crowd, ran men dressed in long gray robes (the hoods of which had holes in them for the eyes and the mouth), carrying a bell in one hand, and a purse in the other, collecting money for the deliverance out of purgatory of the soul of a man who was yet alive.

Among the numerous anecdotes of Pascal Bruno which had been eagerly circulated, the report of his having refused to confess had been very generally spread, and this total disregard of the most essential devotional duty, gave additional weight to the belief so universally entertained of his having entered into a compact with the arch-enemy of mankind in the course of his reckless career.

When he appeared, a feeling of dread

and terror evidently prevailed amongst the spectators, they gazed at the procession with intense interest, but in perfect silence—not a sound, not a cry, not a murmur, was heard to interrupt the service for the dead, which was sung by the Black and White Penitents in the front and rear of the procession. As it proceeded great and increasing crowds followed it to the Marina.

Of all the people present on this eventful morning, Pascal Bruno himself appeared to be the only one not in the slightest degree agitated or excited. He looked at the multitude which surrounded him, with an expression of countenance, equally removed from ostentation and humility, and rather as a man, who, perfectly aware of the duties of individuals towards society, and of society towards individuals, repented as little having violated the one, as he complained of those who had avenged the rights of the other.

The procession halted for a few minutes in the *Place* of the Four Cantons, which forms the centre of the city, for the pressure of the crowd from both sides of the street was so great, that the troops had been forced into the middle of the road, and the leading Penitents were unable to make their way through.

Pascal took advantage of this little check to raise himself up in the cart, in order, as it appeared, to look out for somebody in the crowd to whom he wished to give some parting instructions. But he looked in vain ; and sinking down again upon the truss of straw which served for his seat, his countenance assumed an expression of sorrow and disappointment, which it retained until the procession arrived at the place of execution.

Here the procession made another stop. Pascal again stood up, and having cast a look of perfect indifference at the gallows, which had been erected at the other end of the *Place*, recommenced exploring the vast circle, which seemed paved with heads, with the exception of the terrace of the Prince de Butera, which was totally deserted. His wandering looks, however, at last rested on a rich balcony, hung with damask, and sheltered by a purple canopy. There, on a raised seat, surrounded by the fairest ladies and the noblest lords of Palermo, sat the beautiful Gemma de Castel-Nuovo, who, determined not to

T

deprive herself of the savage pleasure of
beholding the last agonies of her deadly
foe, had established her throne immediately in front of the scaffold.

Gemma looked at Pascal as he approached : their eyes met, and mutually
flashed hatred and vengeance.   Nor had
they ceased to gaze when a loud cry
burst from amongst the crowd who were
nearest the cart.   In an instant Pascal's
countenance not only resumed its former
tranquillity, but wore a new expression
of joy and satisfaction.   The procession
was about to move on, when Pascal, in a
loud and commanding voice, ordered
the train to stop.

The effect of the word given by Pascal was like that of magic.   The whole
crowd seemed nailed to the earth—every
eye was fixed on the bandit.

" What is it?" said the executioner.

" I want to confess," said Pascal.

" You are too late," said the executioner. " Recollect, you yourself sent away the priest."

" My own personal confessor," said Pascal, " is the monk there, on my left, in the crowd. I would have him to shrive me and no one else."

The executioner gave evidence of his impatience, and refused the request; but the moment the people heard that Pascal was ready to accept the services of a priest, a cry of " The confessor! the confessor!" was heard, and the executioner was obliged to consent. The crowd immediately made way for the monk. He was a tall, dark young man, who seemed worn to the bone by the severities of the cloister. He stepped into the cart, and Pascal fell on his knees.

This seemed as a signal to all. In the streets, on the houses, and the balconies at the windows, all the people fell on their knees too; the executioner alone remained on horseback, while his assistants stood by him, as if they were professionally excluded from the general remission of sin. At the same moment the monks began to chant again, in order to drown the sound of Pascal's confession.

"I have looked about for you a long while," said Pascal.

"I waited here," said Ali; for Ali it was.

" I feared that they had broken their promise to me, and that you were to share my fate," said Pascal.

"No, they have kept their word," said Ali. "I am free !"

"Listen !"

"I do."

"Here, on my right," said Bruno, turning to that side, for, his hands being tied, he could not otherwise point out to Ali what he wanted him to see, "you see a balcony hung with cloth of gold ?"

"I do," said Ali.

"On that balcony," said Pascal, "sits a young and beautiful woman, with flowers in her hair. You see *her ?*"

"I do," said Ali. "She is on her knees, praying with the rest."

"That," said Pascal, "is the Countess of Castel-Nuovo."

"She whose window I watched under the night you were wounded ?" said Ali.

"The same," said Pascal. "That woman, Ali, has been the cause of all my sufferings—that woman drove me to commit my first crime—that woman has brought me here."

"Well?" said Ali, anxiously.

"I cannot die in peace," said Pascal, "while I think that woman is to survive me, honoured and happy."

"Then die in peace," said Ali, solemnly.

"Thanks, boy, thanks for that," said Pascal.

"Now, father, one last embrace," said Ali.

The young monk embraced the culprit, as is the custom with priests when they have given their absolution.

"Adieu!" said Ali.

"For ever!" said Pascal. "Now, sirs, forward."

The cortège again was in motion upon the word of Pascal, who gave it, as if he had the right to command. The young monk was lost in the crowd. Every body rose from their knees, and, as the procession advanced towards the scaffold, Gemma reseated herself, while a smile of satisfaction, which she did not seem desirous to conceal, animated her beautiful countenance.

Arrived at the foot of the gibbet, which was formed like the letter H, the cross-bar of which can be raised to the height of the two parallel supporters, the executioner dismounted from his horse and stepped upon the platform, and having hoisted his red flag upon the beam, and ascertained that the rope was properly secured, threw off his coat, in order to give himself greater freedom of action.   Pascal descended from the cart, and declining the attentions of the assistants, who offered their aid, ascended the scaffold, and leant against the ladder which he would have so soon to mount.

At this moment the Penitent who bore the cross stationed himself in front of the culprit, so that he might keep his eyes on it in the last moments of his life; those who had carried the bier seated themselves upon it; and a circle of troops was immediately drawn round the scaffold, leaving within the space only the brotherhood of Penitents, the executioner, his men, and the sufferer.

Pascal mounted the ladder without any assistance, and with as much firmness and calmness as he had exhibited throughout the whole of the dreadful preparations. As the executioner was adjusting the fatal noose, Pascal cast his eyes towards the balcony in which Gemma sat, and a smile of triumphant derision was on his lip. The moment the executioner had slipped the halter round Pascal's neck he seized him round the waist, and threw him violently off the ladder; Pascal fell to the extent of the rope, along which the executioner dexterously slid and threw his whole weight upon his shoulders, while the assistants clung to his legs. The cord, unequal to the weight of the four persons now straining it, snapped asunder, and the whole group lay heaped upon the scaffold. One of them was on his feet in an instant—that was Pascal Bruno. His hands had burst the cords with which they had been originally tied, and he stood before the multitude, bleeding profusely from a wound which the brutal executioner, enraged at the accident, had inflicted with his dagger, which still remained in the right side of the sufferer.

" Miscreant !" said Pascal, addressing him, " you are unworthy to be either an executioner or an assassin. You are neither able to hang nor to murder."

Saying which he tore the reeking poniard from the wound, and plunging it into his heart fell dead upon the spot.

The tumult which then arose was terrific ; many fled from the scene of horror ; others rushed to the scaffold—the body of Pascal was carried off by the Penitents—the executioner barely escaped with his life.

On the evening of this day of blood the Prince de Carini dined with the Archbishop of Montreal, while Gemma, who was not received at the prelate's house, remained at the villa. The evening was as beautiful as the morning had been, and from one of the windows of the room with the blue silk hangings, in which the first scene of our story was enacted, Alicudi was perfectly discernible, and in the far distance beyond, like clouds upon the horizon, the islands of Filicudi and Salina. From the other window there was a beautiful view of the park and gardens, planted with orange-trees, pines, and pomegranates; on the right Mount Pellegrino was visible from its base to its summit, and on the left the view extended nearly to Montreal.

It was at this window that Gemma remained, with her eyes fixed on the ancient residence of the Norman kings, hoping that every carriage she saw coming along the road to Palermo might be that of the Viceroy on his return from the archbishop's; but the shades of evening closed in, and the distant objects melted from her sight, and Gemma, after heaving a sigh that Rodolph should stay so late, finding herself fatigued with the events and excitement of the day, rang her bell for her maid and retired to rest, ordering Gidsa to shut the window which faced the sea, and leave that open which looked to the park, so that she might enjoy the perfume of the orange-flowers which the evening breeze would waft into the room.

It was late before the Viceroy could get away from the hospitable table of the archbishop; indeed the clock of the cathedral, built by William the Good, had struck eleven when his Excellency got into his carriage, in which he was not more than half an hour on the road — five minutes more took him through Palermo to the villa. His first inquiry was after Gemma, who seemed to have gained a double influence over him since her return from her religious seclusion. The answer he received from the Countess's maid was, that her ladyship finding herself fatigued had retired to rest about ten o'clock.

The Prince anxiously proceeded to her room, and endeavoured to open the usual door of entrance, but it was fastened within: he then went round to the door on the second staircase, which was on the other side of the bed, and, as the reader already knows, opened into the recess in which the bed itself stood;

through this he entered gently and cautiously for fear of waking the beautiful sleeper. He paused for a moment to contemplate her beauties slumbering. A single alabaster lamp dimly illumined the apartment, the light of which was so contrived as not to fall upon the eyes of the lovely creature while reposing. The Prince sat down on the side of the bed to gaze on her : she was buried in sleep, and round her neck was twisted the boa which he himself had given her, the dark colour of which more strikingly threw out the beauties of her snow-like skin. The Prince was enchanted with this beautiful statue, for such it looked, indeed the longer he looked the more its total want of animation surprised and alarmed him : he leant over her—he saw that she was strangely pale : he placed his ear near her mouth—he heard no sound—he felt no breath: he took her hand—it was icy cold: he placed his arm round her much-loved body to raise her to the light—he let it fall with a cry of horror! The head of the beautiful Gemma fell from her shoulders and rolled upon the floor.

The next morning the ataghan of Ali was found under the window of the room.

THE END.

ERRATA.

Page 3, line 14 ; for " of," read " by."

P. 84, l. 18 ; for " dare," réad " dared."

P. 179, l. 2 ; for " themselves," read " that island."

P. 188, l. 6 ; for " from," read " of."

P. 196, l. 1 ; for " are," read " is."

P. 209, L. 18 ; for " whom," read " who."

WHITING, BEAUFORT HOUSE, STRAND.

VIII.
V E N E T I A.

By the Author of "Vivian Grey," "Henrietta Temple," &c.

3 vols.

" A work which must extend and strengthen the author's already wide and well-established fame."—*Fraser's Magazine.*

" This story is shaped upon the character of Lord Byron, and some of the events of his life. He figures here as in his own poems, as the hero of the piece; and is introduced, as Lord Cadurcis, at the age of eleven years. His fond, passionate, and inconsistent mother, is also prominent, while Miss Chaworth, somewhat metamorphosed, appears as Venetia Herbert. There is much of poetical beauty and vivid description throughout the volumes. The personal scenes are finely wrought, and the literary topics discussed show much of originality and power.—*Literary Gazette.*

IX.
CAPTAIN MARRYAT'S NEW NOVEL.
SNARLEY YOW; OR, THE DOG FIEND.

Second Edition. In 3 vols. post 8vo.

" Not inferior to any of Captain Marryat's previous works, 'Peter Simple' alone excepted. It is grotesque and humorous from beginning to end."—*Athenæum.*

" This is a work in a completely new style; and full of spirit it is. The dash of historic character gives great effect to the wild and animated narrative."—*Literary Gazette.*

X.
T H E   D I V O R C E D.

BY THE LADY CHARLOTTE BURY.

Authoress of " Flirtation," &c.

2 vols post 8vo. 18s.

" This new novel is one of the most effective of Lady Bury's productions. The story is powerfully and admirably told, and it seems to us that not only is it founded on fact, but that the characters are chiefly drawn from the life."—*John Bull.*

XI.
T H E   P E E R E S S.

Edited by LADY CHARLOTTE BURY.

3 vols.

" This is an extraordinarily clever book. The writer has a great talent for description and the sketching of characters, and is gifted with much sense and judgment. In the course of the work we are introduced to the private lives of Fox, Burke, Sheridan, Lord Grey, and all the illustrious characters of that memorable era, and we are equally familiarized with the galaxy of fashion, when the Prince of Wales was considered the acme of grace and elegance."—*Dispatch.*

XII.
FLITTINGS OF FANCY.
By ROBERT SULIVAN, ESQ.
2 vols. post 8vo.

"Productions of striking grace, tenderness, and romantic interest."—*Court Journal.*
"The vein of originality which characterises Mr. Sulivan's sketches is delightful."—*Literary Gazette.*

XIII.
PICCIOLA;
OR, CAPTIVITY CAPTIVE.
By M. DE SAINTINE.
2 vols. post 8vo. 16s.

"For this beautiful little novel we may venture to predict a degree of popularity in the English world of letters equal to that enjoyed by 'Paul and Virginia,' 'Elizabeth,' and one or two other favourites. It is a production for every class and for every shade of taste."—*Court Journal.*

XIV.
MISS LANDON'S
TRAITS AND TRIALS OF EARLY LIFE.
In 1 vol. neatly bound, price 7s. 6d.

"This exquisite little volume is instinct with all the fascinating attributes of Miss Landon's genius and style. The same grace, the same delicacy, the same pure and feminine feeling, which captivates the imagination in 'Francesca Carrara,' may be traced throughout the 'Traits and Trials of Early Life.'"—*Morning Post.*

XV.
MRS. ARMYTAGE;
OR, FEMALE DOMINATION.
By the Authoress of "Mothers and Daughters."
Second Edition. In 3 vols. post 8vo.

"This is the best of Mrs. Gore's works. The story is new and full of interest."—*Literary Gazette.*
"A clever work, as every thing which comes from Mrs. Gore must be."—*Athenæum.*

XVI.
GENTLEMAN JACK.
A NAVAL STORY.
By the Author of "Cavendish," &c.
3 vols.

"'Gentleman Jack' contains scenes not surpassed by 'Peter Simple.'"—*Liverpool Mail.*

IMPORTANT NEW WORKS.

I.

LIFE OF SIR EDWARD COKE,

LORD CHIEF JUSTICE IN THE REIGN OF JAMES I.,
WITH MEMOIRS OF HIS CONTEMPORARIES.
By C. W. JOHNSON, Esq., Barrister at Law.
In 2 vols. octavo, with Portrait.

II.

MR. BURKE'S HISTORY OF THE LANDED
GENTRY.
A COMPANION TO THE PEERAGE AND BARONETAGE.
Part VIII., price 4s. 6d. To be completed in 16 Monthly Parts,
comprising Accounts of
ALL THE EMINENT FAMILIES IN THE UNITED KINGDOM,
And of upwards of 100,000 Individuals connected with them.
Illustrated with the Armorial Bearings of Each Family, Portraits, &c.

III.

MEMOIRS OF COLONEL CHARLES SHAW,
K.C.T.S.
Late Brigadier-General Spanish Auxiliary Legion, &c.
WRITTEN BY HIMSELF.
And comprising a Narrative of the War in Spain and Portugal,
from its commencement in 1831 to the Dissolution of the
British Legion in June, 1837.
In 2 vols. 8vo. with Portraits of Admiral Napier and Gen. Evans.

"Colonel Shaw writes as a soldier should write, candidly, fearlessly,
and vigorously. His volumes deserve to be read with the deepest attention, as tending to throw an entirely new light on a subject hitherto im-
perfectly understood."—Sunday Times.

IV.

THE SPAS OF GERMANY.
By DR. GRANVILLE.
Author of "Travels to St. Petersburgh," &c.
In 2 vols. 8vo. With Thirty-eight Illustrations.

"Dr. Granville has, in these volumes, given us a full description of the
principal Spas of Germany. We recommend his work, with its numerous
embellishments, to the attention of our tens of thousands of tourists."—
Literary Gazette.

V.

TRAVELS IN CIRCASSIA, KRIM TARTARY,
&c., in 1836-7;

Including a Steam Voyage down the Danube, from Vienna to Constantinople, and round the Coast of the Black Sea.

By EDMUND SPENCER, Esq.

Author of "Germany and the Germans."

In 2 vols. 8vo. with Map of the Black Sea, and Numerous Illustrations, bound.

VI.

THE BENCH AND THE BAR.

By the Author of "Random Recollections of the Lords and Commons, &c.

2 vols. post 8vo.

VII.

THE CITY OF THE SULTAN;
OR, DOMESTIC MANNERS OF THE TURKS.

By MISS PARDOE, Authoress of "Traits and Traditions of Portugal," &c.

2 vols. 8vo., with numerous illustrations.

VIII.

CAPTAIN ALEXANDER'S
NARRATIVE OF A VOYAGE AMONG THE
COLONIES OF WESTERN AFRICA,

IN THE FLAG-SHIP THALIA; AND OF THE KAFFIR WAR OF 1836.

In 2 vols. 8vo., with Maps and Numerous Plates, by MAJOR C. C. MITCHELL, K.H.   32s. bound.

IX.

TRAVELS IN PALESTINE AND SYRIA.
By GEORGE ROBINSON, Esq.

2 vols. post 8vo., with New Maps and Plans.

X.

LORD BROUGHAM'S OPINIONS
ON POLITICS. THEOLOGY, LAW, SCIENCE, EDUCATION, LITERATURE, &c.

WITH MEMOIRS OF HIS LORDSHIP'S LIFE.

In one very thick and closely-printed volume.   12s. bound.

WS - #0039 - 171221 - C0 - 229/152/18 - PB - 9780461163667 - Gloss Lamination

WS - #0039 - 171221 - C0 - 229/152/18 - PB - 9780461163667 - Gloss Lamination